BEING
BELONGING
DOING

Balancing Your Three Greatest Needs

RONALD T. POTTER-EFRON, M.S.W., PH.D.

NEW HARBINGER PUBLICATIONS

Publisher's Note

This publication is designed to provide accurate and authoritative information in regard to the subject matter covered. It is sold with the understanding that the publisher is not engaged in rendering psychological, financial, legal, or other professional services. If expert assistance or counseling is needed, the services of a competent professional should be sought.

Distributed in the U.S.A. by Publishers Group West; in Canada by Raincoast Books; in Great Britain by Airlift Book Company, Ltd.; in South Africa by Real Books, Ltd.; in Australia by Boobook; and in New Zealand by Tandem Press.

Copyright ©1998 by Ronald T. Potter-Efron
New Harbinger Publications, Inc.
5674 Shattuck Avenue
Oakland, CA 94609

Cover design by Poulson/Gluck Design.
Edited by Angela Watrous.
Text Design by Michele Waters.

Library of Congress Catalog Card Number: 97-75472.
ISBN 1-57224-103-9 Paperback

Printed in Canada on recycled paper.

New Harbinger Publications' Website address: www.newharbinger.com

First Edition.

Dedication

Being

To my brothers, Art, Brad, and Don, and to the memory of my mother, Esther, and father, Miles.

Belonging

To all the members of my immediate family: my wife, Pat, and Cindy, Mark, David, Jenny, Jeff, Joshua, and Kristie.

Doing

To my office colleagues at First Things First: Bonnie, Bruce, Carla, Dar, Ed, Jim, Karen, Pat, Ron A., and Trish.

Contents

Acknowledgements

I greatly appreciate the fine people at New Harbinger Publications who have helped bring this book to fruition, in particular my editor, Angela Watrous, who has been able to turn a very personal narrative into a book that is useful to many. Thanks also to Kristin Beck and Matt McKay (and many others at New Harbinger) for having faith that an author whose work has focused mainly on anger could write a "concept" book with a completely different theme.

Several persons have read parts or all of this book, including Eileen Issacson, Mark Scannell, and Pat Potter-Efron. I'm very appreciative of their contributions and encouragement.

Introduction

Some books seem to have a mind of their own, more or less writing themselves, taking their authors in quite unexpected directions. *Being, Belonging, and Doing* is that kind of book.

My original intent was to write a follow-up to *Letting Go of Shame*, a book that my wife, Pat, and I developed several years ago. As I reviewed my materials on shame, I realized that three different kinds of shame stood out: a shame about Being (existential shame), which causes people to feel intrinsically defective, as if there were something terribly and unalterably wrong with them; a shame about Belonging (social shame), in which people believe that others will always reject them; and a shame about Doing (competence or efficacy shame) that makes people feel unnecessarily inept. Three phrases go with these types of shame: "I should not be," "I don't belong," and "I'm not good enough."

I tried dutifully to write that book. But shame is a gloomy emotion, no matter how much hope and optimism you try to pump into it. It's hard to maintain a sense of hope with a focus upon shame. I went through a series of false starts, beginning and stopping, writing one chapter and then another. Indeed, I put the book down twice for months, one time to write *Letting Go of Anger* for New Harbinger and another to write a series of booklets on the angry family for the Johnson Institute in the Twin Cities.

Still, though, this book kept calling. Finally, I heard its voice. This book wasn't meant to be a mere update on shame. Instead, it was supposed to be approached from a broader, more optimistic perspective. *Being, Belonging, and Doing* is really about achieving a particularly satisfying life, one in which we have balanced our basic needs for self-awareness, relationship, and task achievement. Although it is still partly about shame, in that shame affects all three needs, this book is more about pride, joy, and serenity.

It takes a conscious effort for most people to create and maintain that balance. I know I have to think about it every day. As a full-time mental health counselor and part-time writer, I'm particularly prone to "overdoing," a danger that seems quite common these days. Overdoing takes me away from my friends and family, lessening my sense of Belonging. Overdoing also ultimately attacks my very sense of Being. Somehow it's not very satisfying to answer the question, "Who am I?" with, "Well, I'm someone who works twelve hours a day." Of course, I am more than that, but I'll never know what I am as a whole person until I balance my Doing with Being and Belonging.

I hope you will gain several advantages from this book. First, it will be a chance to review a crucial concept—balance. You will probably feel better about yourself when your life is in balance. I use the word "review" here because I think most people already know this deep down. It's just that we forget about what matters most in the rush of getting through each day's business. Secondly, I provide names for three balancing forces: Being, Belonging, and Doing. Names help us organize our experience. Simply asking yourself every day to identify one Being, one Belonging, and one Doing experience will help you more clearly evaluate your level of balance. Thirdly, I provide a number of exercises that can help you develop your awareness and commitment to each area.

Being, Belonging, and Doing has an optimistic theme. I believe almost everyone can gain just by becoming aware of these three aspects of life and the need to balance and coordinate them. It won't take years of therapy, although therapy might help. It will take commitment, common sense, and courage.

Chapter One

Being, Belonging, and Doing:
Our Three Greatest Needs

The Basics

Being: I am. I exist. It is good just to be alive.

Belonging: I connect. I join. I merge with others in partnership, family, friendship, and community. I have a place.

Doing: I work. I play. I find joy in accepting challenges.

Being. Belonging. Doing. These are our three great needs, the three parts of a meaningful and fulfilling life. We are born with these needs. Children instinctively live, bond, and cry different cries in attempt to meet their basic needs.

The basic beliefs regarding Being, Belonging, and Doing that are discussed in this book are:

- We are born with strong needs to be, belong and do.

- Each need must be nurtured, first by the people who raise us and then by ourselves.

- Each need operates somewhat independently from the others. You can be doing well in one and poorly in another.

- Life is most fulfilling when we honor our needs in all three areas.

- The ultimate goal is to balance our needs for Being, Belonging and Doing, so that all three become major aspects of our lives.

Being

✧ Sally is confused and depressed. She has friends, family, and a good job. She should be happy, but she's not:

"Something's wrong. Something's missing. I feel like a phony. It's like I'm living somebody else's life."

Sally's right. She's been a "good girl" all her life, doing exactly what others expect. She's pleased her father by becoming a nurse. She's pleased her mother by raising a family. Her children's needs come first, her husband's second. Sally's needs would come third, if she knew what they were.

"Who am I? What do I want? What do I feel? What do I value?"

Sally is having a problem with Being. ✧

Being: Having an objective reality. Existing. Having an identity. Feeling in harmony with one's inner self.

Being is a difficult word to define. For human beings, the core ideas are that we are alive, we are driven to survive, we are aware that we exist, and that we will eventually cease to be. Being, for a boulder, is a passive experience. A rock exists, but it has no awareness of its own existence. Unfortunately, that's how all too many people approach their own Being. They go through life like thoughtless boulders or, as one person told me, "like a leaf floating on the water, with no mind of my own and no way to steer."

The great tree of life is meant to be grasped and shaken, not merely sat under. The trick is to learn how to turn Being into an active verb: "Here I am, and the world had better get ready for me because I am planning to shake it up a little."

Although it is difficult to define Being, it is easy to describe it. Some of the characteristics of Being are:

- Feeling fully alive and full of energy.

- Living a life that has meaning and purpose.

- Acknowledging and preparing for death.

- Accepting responsibility for your life.

- Listening to your internal voice, even if that means changing the whole course of your life.

- Accepting yourself for who you are.

- Finding who you want to be, not just what others want you to be, and having the courage to follow your own path.

- Appreciating privacy without worrying about getting too lonely. Having an occasional need for solitude. Having the ability to enjoy your own company.

- Seeing life as wonderful. Feeling you don't have to do anything or find a reason to be here. Remembering to enjoy.

- Accepting your special characteristics and differences without shame or embarrassment.

- Maintaining a sense of wonder. Who are you? Who are you becoming?

Belonging

✧ Joe has never once felt he really belonged anywhere. The last-born child in his family, he sensed he was an unwanted burden to his middle-aged parents. Joe didn't talk much at school, so he made few friends. He dated a little but never felt loved. Now he sits in his office at work, eating lunch alone, wondering if he will ever be appreciated. Joe is both alone and lonely.

Joe's main problem in life is Belonging. ✧

Belonging: Union. Attachment. Connection. Love. Friendship. People have a tremendous need to belong with each other. Without Belonging we feel empty and lonely. Something's missing when we cannot join. There are many kinds of Belonging, of course.

We may belong with our family, on a team, with a lover, or to a group. A deep sense of belonging provides warmth and completeness to our lives.

Some of the most important aspects of Belonging are:

- Feeling joy when you share your life.

- Needing to believe you are wanted by others.

- Having a sense of wholeness and completeness.

- Sharing the deepest parts of yourself, including your most private thoughts and feelings.

- Feeling able to say "Yes, I belong."

- Having firm but flexible boundaries to make contact with others without being overwhelmed. "Good fences make good neighbors" (Robert Frost).

- Having the ability to feel both loved (now) and lovable (always).

- Feeling a sense of belonging in nonfamily groups. Having the ability to feel "at home" outside of home.

- Having a spiritual sense that you belong to, with, or in something greater than yourself.

- Feeling assured that there is a place for you in this world.

Doing

✧ Maggie is scared. Recently divorced, she is faced with a thousand jobs her husband used to do. Changing the oil. Paying the bills. Arranging for baby-sitting. The trouble is, she's never thought of herself as a doer. Maggie's avoided the Doing types of responsibility for most of her life: "I just can't do it. Help me." Now there's nobody around to help her. What will she do?

Maggie's facing a crisis around Doing. ✧

Doing: Action. Goals. Work. Play. Engagement. Doing completes our picture, adding a vibrant sense of motion to the canvas of our lives. Can you imagine a life without Doing? Every breath we take is a facet of Doing. So is every step. True, some breaths are labored and many steps are clumsy, but breathe we must. Move we must. Doing is so much a part of living that we take it for granted.

Many of our greatest challenges lay in the sphere of Doing. What should I do? What are my goals? Some significant aspects of doing are:

- Having a general feeling of competence, including the idea that you are pretty good at whatever you choose to do.

- Face life's difficulties. Moving towards your problems instead of avoiding them.

- Participating in all of these five basic processes: choosing, planning, starting, following through, and finishing.

- Remembering that the goal of Doing is to become "good enough," not perfect.

- Being selective about what you do. Doing what feels most right to you will make you the happiest.

- Accepting praise (recognition from others that you can do something well.)

- Reducing self-sabotage (hurting yourself because you cannot handle actually doing something well.) We all probably have a little self-sabotage within us. It's a problem, though, when we regularly "snatch defeat from the jaws of victory."

- Learning from your mistakes instead of giving up.

- Having the ability to stop Doing; reserving time in your life for other things, including Being and Belonging.

The Need to Integrate Being, Belonging, and Doing

✧ Bill is taking a good, long look at his life. He worked seventy-five hours a week until last year when he had a heart attack. Bill made a lot of money. He felt like a smoothly operating machine, a robot. Now all that's over.

"I'm healthy now. I could go back to working every minute. But I need more than that. I want some time just to walk and breathe. I want to go places with my wife before we're too old."

Bill is searching for a new path. He needs to balance work with self-caring and family time. ◇

It's easy to overspecialize in any one of the areas of Being, Belonging, and Doing. Bill, for instance, has concentrated almost all his energy on Doing. That's common in American society, since accomplishment, success, and achievement are so highly rewarded. It's also possible to get overinvolved with Belonging. You can get so wrapped up in family, for example, that you lose track of yourself. Finally, people can get too focused on Being. "Who am I?" can become an obsession, to the point where people cut themselves off from work and productive activity in futile pursuit of themselves, much like a dog chasing its own tail.

Being, Belonging, and Doing belong together. They can, and perhaps must, be studied separately, because each is substantially different from the others. The goal, however, is to balance these three, which can result in a remarkably more fulfilling life. These three components are the three most important needs of our lives. They are part of us at birth and stay with us until we die. They are like three differently colored fabrics waiting to be woven together by you to make your own personal tapestry. The rich purple of Being. The warm yellow of Belonging. The bright red of Doing. Each is beautiful in its own right. Together, they are breathtaking.

Whispers and Shouts

Being, Belonging, and Doing. Individually, each calls for your attention, sometimes softly like a tiny bird's first call in the morning. You can barely hear the cooing in the background, drifting out of the silence. Will you listen and follow? Or will you ignore the call because you're too busy with other things? It lets you decide.

At other times, your needs call out like a jackhammer. "Hey, you, I said *pay attention to me.* I won't let you ignore me any longer." That's when your previously peripheral Being, Belonging, or Doing needs surge to the forefront of your awareness. That's when you simply must stop what you've been focusing on long enough to pick up the dropped fabric of Being, Belonging, or Doing and add it to your tapestry.

You may hear whispers as you read this book. You may hear shouts. Either way, take the time to listen, and perhaps you will understand yourself better. You may discover where you most need to concentrate your energy right now. Remember that the goal is to help you balance these three central forces so that your life can be as satisfying as possible.

Chapter Two

The Bliss of Being

Self-Awareness

I am. I exist. What remarkable statements. The self aware of itself.

As far as we know, probably only humans and a few great apes can see themselves in the mirror and understand what they are seeing. "Hey, that's me! I have brown eyes, black hair, dimples. There's the scar on my hand from the time the knife slipped a few years ago." We, as humans, have the remarkable ability to notice that we are alive. We've developed a true sense of self. We know we exist as one person over time, awake or asleep, happy or sad, in sickness or in health. I am and I know I am.

We're even better than that. We are constantly personally evolving. We are constantly becoming. The unaware infant becomes the two-year-old who knows it's their birthday party. The two-year-old becomes the middle-school child absorbed in play, practicing for adulthood. The child becomes the teenager who desperately wants the independence they are still not ready for. The teen becomes the young adult struggling to find their place in the world. The young adult grows into a working, family raising middle-ager. The middle-ager grows old and, hopefully, wise. That's why the mere statement "I am" is outdated the moment you say it. "I am" is simply the meat in the sandwich between "I was" and "I will be."

Self-awareness is a mixed blessing. We know all too well of our mortality. As my friend, Ray Dreitlein, says, the only thing we can be certain of in this life is that none of us will make it out alive. We worry about our health. We worry about how we will die. We may urgently want to live forever, even though we know full well that this is impossible. Some of us turn to religion or spirituality for relief, to lessen our fears of death with the wonderful promise of eternal bliss.

Emotional pain is an inevitable companion to self-awareness. We all suffer grave disappointments. The would-be artist discovers they cannot master perspective. The new parent has to drop out of school to provide for their family. Loved ones leave, voluntarily or not, and you are deeply wounded. These pains may be so great you may vow never to try again, never to hope again, never to love again. Seeking safety, you can fail to notice that you are becoming dry and stale like a discarded loaf of bread. The self needs challenges to thrive. Emotional pain turns out to be both inevitable and necessary to grow. In the words of Khalil Gibran, "The deeper sorrow carves out your being the more joy you can contain."

The purpose of this chapter is to help you celebrate your Being. You exist. You are. You are becoming.

Bliss

Bliss is the name for the special feeling that we have when we allow ourselves to fully celebrate Being. Bliss is a marvelous emotion, the world's best antidepressant, a natural high that makes life worth living.

Bliss is the Being state of joy. Bliss is defined in some dictionaries as "complete happiness." Other terms that hint of the Being state of joy are ecstasy, rapture, beatitude, enchantment, and wonderment. These words all point to the experience of Being completely and joyfully involved in one's present experience, freed from anxiety, absolutely full of life.

You must be free (for the moment) to feel bliss. Free from worry about the past. Free from concerns about the future. Free from all the "shoulds" and "musts" that keep you from discovering the moment. Free from expectations, obligations, and duties. Of course, nobody stays free from these concerns for long. They are a normal and necessary part of life. Still, bliss is a state of inner contentment and is not compatible with simultaneous fear and anxiety.

Bliss is a state of enlightened contentment. Blissful experiences may involve pleasure, but pleasure is not the primary sensation. Rather, the blissful person is serene, at peace with oneself and the world. Bliss brings a tremendous inner joy. The state of bliss may also be deeply spiritual, coming from the sense that there is a higher beauty in oneself and in all things.

Bliss is to experience the moment. Don't get distracted. Be here now. Feel your body's energy. You are alive. You are alive! Let yourself be.

The Fortune of Feeling Bliss

Psychology is a world of trends and fashions. Recently there has been a good deal of parent bashing, partly for good reasons. As a full-time mental health therapist, I've seen a lot of badly hurt adults who did indeed have terrible childhoods. Somehow they survived, though, as have the many, many adults who grew up in relatively healthy homes. This leads me to the idea that sometimes, while a person's parents may not have been ideal, their parents were good enough.

What, exactly, do "good enough" parents do? Mostly, they pay positive attention to their children. They coo at their infants as they feed them and change diapers. They take a little time to play trains and dolls with their young ones. They listen to their stories, even when they don't make sense. They bandage their physical wounds and calm their fears. They praise their children, early and often. They tell their children in a thousand ways, both verbally and nonverbally, "You are. I'm so glad you're alive. I'm interested in you so it's okay for you to be interested in yourself, too." They hold their children. They comfort them. They celebrate their existence.

Good enough parents affirm their children: You are good.

Good enough parents comfort their children: You are safe.

Good enough parents are interested in their children: Show me. Tell me.

Good enough parents help their children feel good enough themselves. Alive. Aware. Capable of bliss.

I'm a grandparent now, so I've had a chance to evaluate my parents' parenting style, my own, and my children's. Here's my conclusion: we do the best we can under very difficult conditions. Raising children is amazingly hard work. There is no sure way, so we have to guess a lot. We make a lot of mistakes, too, like the time I forgot my six-year-old son at the supermarket. Luckily, my children haven't noticed only my mistakes. If they did, they would probably never talk to me again.

If you are capable of bliss, you undoubtedly had someone in your life who loved you and showed interest in you. Maybe not all the time, maybe not even most of the time, but often enough for you to feel periods of contentment. Those moments helped you discover that you are both valued and valuable as a human Being.

Most people do feel moments of bliss—times when they are simply Being. These are periods, however brief, when you feel good about yourself. Moments of celebration. Moments of certainty. I am and that is good. I am and that is enough. Sure, there may be a few shadowy doubts creeping around the edges of your mind even then, but they are far in the background. Right now you are alive and well. Thank everyone, family and nonfamily, who cherished you and celebrated your existence. Their love and interest in you is what helped you become the self you are, and allow you to experience the bliss of Being.

Characteristics of Confident Being

Confident Being is different from being confident. Being confident is something specific: "I am confident that I can make French toast." It may even be a general attitude towards doing things: "I am confident I can do almost anything well." In other words, Being confident is mostly about Doing.

Confident Being, on the other hand, focuses on who you are, not on what you can do. Confident Being means you are certain your life has value: "I am and that is good." Contrast this with deeply shamed people who think their very existence is a waste of time. Contrast confident Being, too, with doubters who hope maybe they can "just be" but lack certainty. Lacking confidence, they may try to convince everyone they are good by taking care of others and neglecting themselves. Deep down, though, they may always wonder if they will ever be good enough without having to do these things.

What is it like to have confident Being? Naturally, the feeling is different in each of us. The experience of confident Being is as unique as Being itself. However, the sensation can be described in general terms. Before going forward, though, remember not to keep score. The goal is not to worry about how close to perfect you are. It is to help you find the sometimes hidden path towards personal contentment.

Certainty of Being

First, people with confident Being have certainty of Being. They simply know they exist and they have a reason to be. Their existence is so intrinsic that they don't have to prove or justify their existence. "I am" is a given. This helps them tolerate the basic anxieties of life. Of course, they have their fair share of fundamental human fear and pain. They shiver in the cold winds of loss and disappointment like everyone else. They are fully aware of their mortality as well. However, that doesn't keep them from celebrating the simple fact they are alive.

Sense of Wonder

Ever notice how curious little kids are? "What's this? What's that?" The world is a place to explore, full of fascinating stuff. Who wants to take a nap when there are dogs' tails to pull, falling leaves to catch, hundreds of combinations of bread and jam, and tiny feet longing to wander?

People with confident Being are genuinely interested in themselves. They see themselves as an unfolding mystery: "What's today's segment going to look like? What's the name of tomorrow's chapter?" They aren't obsessed with themselves, however. They don't worry about disappearing into nothingness if they take their eyes off themselves for awhile. They are just as interested in others as themselves, in "Who are you?" as well as "Who am I?" People with confident Being are simply alert to the great adventure of the journey of life. Their sense of wonder helps them participate fully in their inner and outer worlds.

Taking Responsibility

Those with confident Being take full responsibility for their own lives. They absolutely refuse the victim stance: "I am personally responsible for my happiness," they insist. "Sure, bad things have happened to me. But that's true for everyone. Nobody gets through life without pain and suffering. I could choose to be miserable forever because of my suffering, but I don't. Instead, I create my own happiness. It's entirely up to me to be joyful and serene."

Taking responsibility for your own life is never simple. It takes courage. You must be brave to accept the idea that only you can make you happy. It's so much easier to wait, like an open-mouthed baby bird, for others to feed and nurture you. But that stance inevitably brings disappointment and bitterness. First off, others don't always bring you enough worms to fill your belly. Besides, sometimes the ones they do bring taste funny. It's better to fly from that nest of weakness and irresponsibility so you can find your own food.

Being Unique

Each of us is special, different, unique. The more confident Being we have the more we can accept the differences that set us apart from others.

Let me tell you a true story. One day a few years ago I was complaining to John, my therapist, that I felt different from everybody else in Eau Claire, Wisconsin. I'm Jewish, they're not. I'm short, they're tall. I'm introverted, they're extroverted. Etc., etc., etc. I'm different. I don't fit in. It's awful.

John listened to my complaints for a few minutes. Then he looked at me and said: "Ron, you're right. You are different. What's wrong with that? Why don't you accept your differences and just get on with living here in Eau Claire?"

Good question. I had gotten hung up on the problem of Being different. Instead, John invited me just to accept the fact of difference. Of course I'm different. So is everybody. What's the big deal? I was a tad short in the area of confident Being that day. I needed help understanding and remembering that I am unique and special, just like everyone else. Just like you.

Being Alone

Those with confident Being enjoy Being alone from time to time. They seek out privacy and solitude. They'll explore going alone to a movie or a restaurant, for example. They may even go off on a solo camping trip, declining contact with others for several days or weeks. It's not that they hate people. Rather, they want time to reconnect with themselves.

Confident Being allows people to move gracefully between the states of "alone" and "together." They truly enjoy friendship, but they are not compulsive joiners. They embrace aloneness without becoming hermits. Above all, they don't suffer much from what Clark Moustakas called "loneliness anxiety," the fear of being alone that drives people away from themselves. Being alone is a part of life they can enjoy without excess anxiety.

Challenges to Confident Being

The formula for a good life is deceptively simple. Just be. That's it, at least in the area of Being I am currently describing. Unfortunately, just Being is difficult. A thousand barriers interfere. Being may be a quiet, beautiful path, but it's strewn with massive boulders.

Some of those rocks are old and gray, the products of childhood stresses and conflicts. Others look suspiciously fresh. Those are the stones you've personally thrown in your own path. They're the adult blocks to Being from your more recent past and present. The conglomerates are the largest boulders, though. They're the ones that began forming in your childhood, only to have you add a few new layers of your own as adults. For example, if the message in the center of one conglomerate is, "You're not worth looking at," courtesy of Mom or Dad, the outside reads, "I'm not worth looking at," courtesy of yourself.

There are many conditions that help people gain confident Being. As a child, people need parents who show them love, respect, and interest. They need caregivers who celebrate their existence and encourage them to grow into themselves, whomever that may be. These are parents who understand that their children aren't their clones, put upon the earth only to be like them.

Grown-ups thrive under the same conditions. Love, respect, and interest bring out our true selves at any age. However, we must add a new ingredient by the time we reach adulthood. Self-love, self-respect, and self-interest now become as important as positive attention from others. What good does it do, for example, to have your employer tell you how much you are appreciated when you feel like a slacker or fraud?

There are many, many challenges to confident Being. I'll name and describe several of the most common ones.

False Modesty

✧ Deion's met a nice woman named Harmony. He's thinking of going out with her seriously. The only problem is he can't get her to talk about herself at all.

"Who are you?" he asks.

"Oh, I'm just me," she answers with a shrug.

Deion tells Harmony he really wants to know who she is. What are her values? Her goals? Her wants? Her needs? Harmony won't tell, though, because her parents taught her that speaking about yourself is wrong. They taught her not to be curious about herself and to never be the center of attention. Harmony actually feels guilty when she's noticed. Her rule is to go through life as quietly and inconspicuously as possible. The fact is, she can't answer Deion's questions because she's never allowed herself to take the time to think about them. ✧

Most people who won't talk about themselves believe that it is somehow bad to do so. They've learned that it's "prideful" to think or talk too much about themselves. Women are especially trained this way. All too many people, especially women, shamefully reject their own self-awareness, confusing healthy awareness with immodesty and pride.

I have a name for this prohibition: false modesty. That's when you turn away from yourself, unnecessarily, thinking that not noticing who you are and what you want is virtuous. The costs of false modesty are high. First, you harm yourself by not knowing what you most want and need. Secondly, you hurt others by not giving them the gift of your real self.

But don't we live in an era of rampaging narcissism? Isn't everyone selfish? Self-centered? Totally absorbed in their own Woody Allen–style neurotic monologues? Shouldn't the message for today be to get out of your own head and pay more attention to others?

For some people, yes, that's true. For others, particularly those who have lost track of themselves somewhere along the way, no. For all those women and men who feel bad about paying any attention to themselves, no, no, no. It's time for you to become curious about yourselves. In fact, it's way past time to learn about yourself and share your new knowledge with those you care about. The book that contains the story of your life has been waiting in your library for years. Now is the time to pick it up and read it. It won't hurt one bit, either, to let others take a peek.

Self-Neglect

Self-neglect is closely related to disinterest. The disinterested person says: "I'm not worth thinking about." Self-neglecters say "I'm not worth caring about." Self-neglecters believe they are like an old car ready to be taken to the junkyard. Why bother spending time and money on a broken-down piece of trash?

So they don't. They forget to make that doctor's appointment they've been putting off forever. They eat whatever's in the refrigerator without thinking about their health. Sure, it would be great to exercise, but they just won't take the time. It's not that they necessarily hate their bodies, though. That's too strong a feeling. Rather, they are too involved with other things. They put self-care so far down on their mental priority list that they never get to it. "I'll get around to me later" all too often becomes "never."

Self-neglecters don't only ignore their bodies. They'll fail to put money away for retirement. They'll fix up other people's houses but not paint their own. Whatever they could do for themselves, they don't. Too much of a bother.

What's the cure for self-neglect? Giving yourself permission to be important. Making a commitment to treat yourself as decently as you treat others. Paying attention to your wants and needs and then taking immediate action to meet those needs.

False Self

Many excellent psychologists (Winnicott, Masterson, Johnson) have been writing for years about the false self. The false self develops as a child renounces parts of themselves their parents don't like. Simultaneously, they exaggerate more acceptable parts of their personality.

✧ Mandy, a typical three-year-old, loved to cuddle and play with dolls. Unfortunately, that's when her father suddenly abandoned the family. Mandy's mother soon became bitter and depressed. She also decided her daughter was too soft and vulnerable. Not wanting her daughter to suffer, Mom decided to toughen her up. "No more dolls. No more cuddles. This world's a hard place. Only the strong survive. Throw away those dolls and quit your crying."

Mandy learned quickly. She discovered an aggressive, cold part of her that her mother appreciated. She buried her softness in a box far back in her mind, becoming tougher and meaner and colder and stronger every year. She was good at what she did. Very good. She grew up to be an "ice queen," distant and aloof. She married and had children, teaching them the same lessons about life she had learned from her mother.

But something felt wrong. Mandy kept feeling the urge to cuddle with her children or show more warmth to them than she was used to. She kept trying to push back these desires, her mother's words still influencing her actions, but her desire to have more closeness wouldn't go away. That's when she showed up in counseling, confused and scared.

Mandy had developed a false self. She even felt sometimes that she was living somebody else's life. And she was. She had grown an identity that met the needs of her mother but not her own. It took her about a year to reclaim her softer side. She had to give herself permission to be the person she wanted to be, her true self, rather than to keep limiting and editing herself. ✧

We all make compromises with reality. We play roles. We become what others want us to be. All that's part of the social contract. Still, we need to take the time to seek out and honor our real selves.

The questions for those who feel they've developed a false self to ask themselves are these: What parts of yourself have you discarded? Ignored? Refused to accept? Run from?

Self-Hatred and Self-Destructiveness

✧ "I hate myself. I should die."

Thus speaks Billy, a nine-year-old with lots of problems. Attention Deficit Disorder. Depression. Learning disabilities. Billy has trouble getting along with his schoolmates. He fights a lot with his sister. He can't obey his parents' rules. Some days it seems like nobody likes Billy, including Billy. ✧

Who knows how many Billys there are in this world, men and women of all ages who simply despise themselves and wish they were dead. Some may be depressed and need professional help. Many are going through a crisis and will soon like themselves better. Others, though, have a deep inner conviction that they are so bad they should die.

Are people born this way? Most often not. More frequently they grow up in shaming households, the kind in which there is little praise and massive criticism. Somewhere along the line they threw their lot in with the enemy. They began to agree that they were fundamentally flawed, irretrievably broken. The natural conclusion from there is to believe they should die. They may actually attempt suicide to kill their body, or they may instead kill their souls through alcoholism or addiction. Most often, though, they settle upon calling themselves terrible names and thoroughly berating themselves for staying alive.

Self-hatred is a strong acid on the soul. It eats at the center of one's Being, the sense that life is a great gift to be used and enjoyed. I believe that self-hatred can be changed. Certainly a nine-year-old like Billy shouldn't have to live the rest of his life feeling miserable about himself. Nobody should—whatever their age. But healing self-hatred is a slow, slow process. One big step is to embrace the idea that every person, including you, simply deserves to be. It's not a matter of Being good or bad, because good and bad are judgment calls. There is no judgment in the phrase "I am."

Doubting the Right to Exist

✧ Marti is a walking apology. She never feels good enough. She never thinks she can just be. Instead, her formula for life is to work very hard. That way, maybe others will at least tolerate her. She never believes they will ever really accept her.

Marti has a double problem. She doesn't think she's good enough to be or to belong. That only leaves doing. And so she works. Hour after hour, day after day, to the point of total exhaustion. It's not that she loves putting in all that overtime at her job. Nor does she love to be the family chauffeur, seamstress, cook, and wall washer. She's simply afraid to stop and exist because then she's sure her boss would fire her, her husband would divorce her, and her children would never talk with her again. Marti is a doer by default. It's her only option. ✧

There are many Martis in this world. They suffer a crisis in confidence because they really don't know how to be. Their lives are spent in perpetual bargaining: "If I'm good, will you let me stay? Will I be good enough if I work hard?"

The key to recovery for Marti is self-acceptance. She needs to learn that she is worthwhile just as she is. Sure, it's important to do good things. But doing good things can't make you feel worthwhile deep inside. She needs to say this: "World, here I am. Take me or leave me. This is me. I'm glad I'm alive. I won't apologize any longer for Being myself." Of course, it would sure help if she would believe what she says.

Excessive Fear or Avoidance of Death

Charles Whitfield asks this question: "Regarding my death, do I feel prepared and unafraid?" Being implies nonbeing. Life implies death. Nevertheless, it takes great courage to live with real awareness of our eventual demise.

Many people simply ignore their mortality as long as they can. For instance, a few years ago my wife Pat and I led a training group of professional and student counselors. One job we gave them was to walk around the neighborhood, just Being alive and taking in the sights and sounds.

These people were good. They scoured the neighborhood. They saw everything. They heard everything. Except that only one of them walked through the nursing home right next door. The rest avoided it. Why? Likely because they didn't want to see older people and start thinking about death. Regarding their deaths, these people are not very well prepared.

Others obsess about death. They think about it all the time. Death, death, death. They usually try to fight death as hard as they can, through diet, exercise, magic. Death is the enemy, the dark terror that comes in the night. Regarding their death, these people are afraid.

Being is enhanced when you can face death prepared and unafraid. You prepare by increasing your awareness of mortality and by fighting through the natural tendency to deny death. You become unafraid by finding meaning and purpose in the life you lead and spiritual connection with the universe.

Avoidance of Solitude

How long can you be alone before you start getting anxious? An hour? A day? A week? A month? A year? Forever? Many people avoid solitude because they associate it with loneliness. Solitude is chosen, positive, pleasant, and educational, as opposed to loneliness, which is unchosen, negative, unpleasant, scary, and sad. Yet both refer to the state of being alone.

The more you embrace your Being the easier it is to stand alone. Think of the difference between "I hate Being alone. I don't even like myself," and "I enjoy being alone. I'm my own best friend." In fact, one of the best ways to practice Being is to seek solitude.

I'm not saying that healthy people shouldn't need anybody. The goal, after all, is to find balance between Being, Belonging, and Doing. Being without Belonging would be as empty as Belonging without Being. But one marker of confident Being is comfort with aloneness.

Excessive Need for Attention and Affirmation

"Pay attention to me!"

How about that for a basic need? Infants couldn't survive without physical attention, of course. But they also need emotional attention, parents and caregivers who take an interest in their Being.

People with confident Being say, "I am."

People who are insecure about their Being say, "I think I am. I hope I am. Am I?" They turn to others to confirm their existence: "Yes, you are." Now that's a perfectly normal process for a young child who is just learning he or she exists. But what happens when an adult needs constant affirmation of their existence?

⬦ Tedra is a smart, talented, and attractive twenty-five-year-old woman. But inside she feels like she's falling apart, as if she has no "glue" to hold her together. That's why she calls her lover, Brad, about five times a day, to get reassurance that she's worthy of Being. Brad feels stifled and overwhelmed by Tedra's neediness, but he doesn't know what to do. Tedra tells him that she can't make it without hearing his comforting voice—she'd fall apart. Tedra needs Brad to confirm her very existence.

He's become the glue that holds her together. Because of this, Brad sometimes feels more like her father than her lover. ✧

Tedra needs to find her own glue. That's the only way she can have healthy relationships and be secure enough to spend time alone. That's not an easy task for an adult who is used to using others for constant affirmation, but it is possible. People in Tendra's situation will probably need counseling, though, to help get them started.

Drifting

Nelson is scared. Eight months ago he learned that the plant he's worked at for the last twenty-five years would soon close down. Since then, many of his co-workers have left voluntarily, accepting early retirement or heading toward other jobs or schools. Not Nelson. He's never made a major decision about his life. He's just drifted along, working at the plant where his brother got him a job, marrying and having a family because that's what people did. He's been on automatic pilot so long he's forgotten how to steer his own life.

Author Irving Yalom writes that we face four major tests of our Being: mortality, aloneness, meaning, and choice. All four areas raise questions about Being. Can I accept my death? Can I handle my aloneness? What is the meaning of my life? What are my choices? Having covered the first two questions already in this chapter, let's focus on the others.

Actually, I believe that the last two issues are almost the same. The meaning of your life consists of the choices you make. What will you have for breakfast today? Who will you vote for in the next election? Will you choose to vote? How fast will you drive to work? Are you going to have children? Will you stay in the marriage or seek a divorce? Go on to school? Have a drink? Quit smoking? Read this book? Roll up your answers to all these choices and the hundreds more you make each day—that is the meaning of your life. Your choices are what define your Being.

People with confident Being are more aware of their choices than those who are less confident. That doesn't mean they like having to make choices. Choice-making may fill them with fear and anxiety, but they still make those choices because that's part of Being.

Here's a few questions: What choices are you facing? Have you been avoiding any significant choices, the kind that could greatly affect your life? If so, why?

Drifting through life can lessen your sense of Being. Asking yourself these questions is one way to stop drifting and start steering. But steering, of course, takes courage: the courage to look deeply into yourself, the courage to make changes in your life that will add to your long-run satisfaction, the courage to be.

The exercises that follow will help you to get to know better the Being aspects of your life. They will probably be both enjoyable and exciting, especially if you let yourself take the time and energy to complete them fully and deeply. Gaining self-awareness about your Being is a good way to become your own best friend.

Exercises to Help You Be

Exercise—Who Am I?

Sit down with a piece of paper and try to answer the following question at least ten times: "Who am I?" Take your time. Approach the question each time as if it is the first. Search deep within yourself for some less obvious answers.

If this was a tough test for you, remember that it gets easier the more you embrace your Being. By the way, it's okay if you reached the point of answering, "I don't know" to this question. Just stay curious and interested and eventually you'll probably be able to answer the question more thoroughly. Once you can answer the question ten different ways, try answering this question ten times: Who am I becoming?

Exercise—Spending Time Alone

Would you like a quick opportunity to get to know yourself better? Here's what to do: During the next week do one thing every day alone that you would normally do with others. Go to a movie, restaurant, ball game, shopping, or church by yourself. Take a drive in the country. Spend twenty-four hours by yourself—without books, music, or writing equipment if you really want a challenge.

Exercise—Choices

Keep a notebook with you and write down all the choices you make during the next twenty-four hours: To eat or not, to make love or not, to shout or whisper, to work or play.

These are your basic yes-or-no choices. But also notice your other choices: how, when, where, with whom, how much, what kind. You'll probably be amazed at not only how many choices you make every day but also at how many things you do without really choosing. Avoiding choices is the perfect formula for making life meaningless. Avoiding choices is a Being block. It leads to depletion, depression, and despair. On the other hand, becoming aware of your choices and then making conscious decisions about them creates meaning in life.

Exercise—From Self-Hate to Self-Love

People who suffer from self-hate need to travel on a long journey. They start out at self-hate and gradually move toward self-love. But there are many stops along the way: I hate myself . . . I dislike myself . . . I tolerate myself . . . I'm neutral toward myself . . . I treat myself like a casual acquaintance . . . I'm beginning to like myself . . . I'm a good friend to myself . . . I'm my best friend . . . I love myself.

To get yourself to self-love, you need to first ask yourself some questions. Where are you on this journey? Which direction are you moving? What will it take for you to get to the next stop? What does it mean to you to be a friend to yourself? A best friend? What does it mean to you to feel true love for yourself?

Exercise—Wandering

The goal of this exercise is to help you discover or rediscover the basic joy of Being. All you have to do is go outside, preferably to a place where there aren't a lot of people, and wander around. Let your feet take you wherever they desire. Don't set any specific goals or directions. This isn't the time to go to the store for groceries. The goal is to really notice what goes on around you all the time that you are often too busy to notice. Here are the guidelines:

1. Go outside and start wandering, letting your feet take you wherever they wish. Don't set any particular places to go or things to do.

2. As you wander, notice anything and everything that asks for your attention: birds calling, leaves falling, the wind in your face, the smell of a flower, etc.

3. Stop for awhile when something "calls" to you. Really pay attention to it with all your senses. See, hear, touch, smell, and taste—make rich and deep contact.

4. Notice your thoughts and feelings as you make contact. Are you fully aware and alive? Are you blocking the experience in some way? If so, try letting go of the distractions for a minute so you can fully experience your Being.

5. When you are ready, say good-bye to whatever has occupied your attention. Continue wandering.

6. Keep going for thirty minutes or an hour. Then go home and compare this experience of Being with your normal life. How could you build in more opportunities to let yourself be like this?

Exercise—Reconnecting with Your Body

It's easy in this psychological age to forget that the word feeling, as in "what are you feeling right now?" literally refers to what is going on in your body. Being is to be connected with your body—to become aware of the physical sensations that eventually get translated into words like sad, mad, glad, and scared.

There are many ways to reconnect with your body. Breathing exercises and relaxation training are very helpful. Directions for breathing and relaxation exercises can be found in many books, such as *The Relaxation and Stress Reduction Workbook*.

Keeping a feelings and sensations journal is another method to reconnect with your body. This kind of journal will be particularly useful to you if you tend to live from the neck up, paying a lot of attention to your thoughts but often ignoring your body.

Directions: Take a small pad of paper with you. Whenever you get a chance, but no less than once an hour, ask yourself what bodily sensations you are having right now. Write them down and see if you can connect these sensations with an emotion or feeling. Pay special attention at times when you are most likely to have distinct feelings, such as when someone says they love you, gives you praise, or disagrees with you. Write down the situation in your journal. Here's an example:

3:00 P.M. Called George. He offered to make dinner. Body: warm, smiling. Name: happy.

6:00 P.M. Sudden overtime. Can't go home for dinner. Body: stomach tense, making fists, breathing fast. Name: anxious? angry?

9:00 P.M. Home from work. George angry. Body: trembling a little, short breaths. Name: upset.

Try doing this exercise for about a week. Then review your responses. Look for patterns such as these: a general deadening or insensitivity to your body that keeps you from feeling much of anything; specific sensation blocks that allow you to notice some feelings but not others; oversensitivity to some or all feeling sensations. The goal here is to become aware of how your body and mind are connected. However, you may want to do more if you become aware of a strong feelings block or oversensitivity. Contact a good feelings- and body-oriented therapist for help if you decide to go further in this area.

Exercise—In Search of Your Real Self

You'll need two sheets of unlined paper and some crayons, colored pencils, or felt pens. You don't need to be an artist to do this, so try not to judge the exercise as a work of art.

Directions:

1. Draw your mask on one sheet of paper—what you let the rest of the world see about who you are. It can be straightforward (a smiley face) or symbolic (one person drew a table because: "People think they can pile up anything they want on me and I'll always have room for more."). Your mask shouldn't be judged as good or bad. It's the part of you that is safest for you to show others.

2. Then take the second sheet of paper and draw the person behind your mask. Take your time with this figure. Put down what is really there, not what you wish were there or what you think others would like to see there. Sometimes more than one image comes to mind under your mask. If so, draw each image separately.

3. Place the mask on top of the other picture(s). Think about what you say, do, and feel when you are wearing your mask. Then look at the other picture(s) and ask yourself the same questions.

People who spend too much time with their masks on often feel like they are missing something important. They have a false self in that they cannot connect with the person beneath the mask. The real self, however, is not just the person under the mask. Your real self is a combination of the self you show others (your mask) and all of the pictures underneath.

The act of Being is never completed while we live. We are constantly growing and changing, continually becoming as well as Being. But, paradoxically, that is exactly why we must attend to our Being in the present. Soon, this particular instant of Being will be over, never to be felt again. Failing to capture this moment of Being, we will lose forever whatever personal experience and wisdom is available right now.

The need to be, however, is only part of our meaningful existence. Being must be balanced with our other needs, specifically Belonging and Doing. The next chapter focuses upon our need to belong.

Chapter Three

We Long to Belong

The Need to Attach

We long to belong. We need closeness. Comfort. Intimacy. Union. But why? What's so important about connection that makes people sacrifice opportunities, independence, and preferences for the people and communities they feel connected to? There are two basic sources of Belonging, two swift-moving motivational streams that combine to form a deep and powerful river. One, the need to attach, emerges at birth. The second, sexuality, develops more gradually and doesn't fully emerge until adolescence.

The infant's need to belong is rooted in one concept: survival. From the moment of birth that child depends upon others for food and comfort. "I need you" is a physical and emotional reality. Poor helpless thing? Hardly! Nature has provided that newborn babe with a tremendous tool. It's called bonding.

Let me give a personal example. I was about twenty years old when Pat gave birth to our first child, Cindy. Those were the old days when fathers weren't permitted in the delivery room, so I did the traditional wait-and-worry number. After several hours the word came: all was well with mother and child. Still, I couldn't come in to see Pat or Cindy. So I waited, staring impatiently at the door to the delivery area. Then came the miracle. The door opened. There was my daughter being taken to the nursery. By chance Cindy's eyes were open and just happened to meet mine. Suddenly I felt one of the strongest sensations I've ever had. It was emotional tunnel vision. All I could see was her. All I could feel was her. I was filled with something even stronger than love, something that brought me to tears. It took all of about five seconds and I was hooked for life. This was my child and I would take care of her from now on. She needed me. I needed her. We became irrevocably bonded in that brief moment.

Miracle? Yes. Unusual? Well, no. It's happened to me twice again, with the births of Jenny and Josh. It's happened to millions of mothers and fathers over the centuries. In fact, it's unusual (and ominous) when this particular miracle doesn't occur between parents and children. The name for this miracle is bonding. The result is attachment, the strongest physical and emotional connection between people.

Children's attachment has been studied in depth for years, most notably by John Bowlby and Mary Ainsworth. They discovered that the power of attachment isn't constant. Mostly, it lies quietly, like a well-burped baby after a satisfying meal. "I love you," coos Mom. "I'm full," murmurs Baby. They're both content.

If only life were this simple. But sooner or later that baby will start squalling. I'm hungry. Thirsty. Need a diaper change. There's something wrong and you're going to hear about it. So, too, with attachment. Something always goes wrong for one basic reason. Each of us is separate. No one can be there every minute of the day for someone else. Children catch on to this fact around the end of their first year. They hate it. They fight it. They fear it. Try sneaking out for a movie. They'll spot you every time. Sure, Grandma is there. But she's not Mom. She's not Pop. Get ready for a loud protest, a "How can you do this to me?" that is almost certain to trigger your guilt. According to Bowlby and Ainsworth, protest is followed by despair (a temporary physical and emotional collapse), followed by acceptance (getting on with life). The whole process takes about three minutes with a baby. It can take years with an adult going through a major separation such as the death of a parent or a divorce.

Separation anxiety is the basic, instinctive Belonging fear. What will happen if you go away? How will I survive? Fortunately, a child's separation anxiety is usually relieved quickly. Dad and Mom come back and hold them, comforting and reassuring. A child gradually learns a very important lesson: "The people I love, the people who love and comfort me, want to be with me. They may leave from time to time, but then they return. Good-byes may never become great fun, but when a good-bye leads to the promise of a hello in the not-too-distant future, it becomes a whole lot less painful."

Children become grown-ups who struggle with their own abandonment issues. Good-byes can be difficult to say and to hear. Doubts sneak in. So do jealousy and demands for reassurance. "Sure, go out and have a great time," says the confident adult. "No, don't leave me!" screams the insecure inner child. "I love you and have total faith in you," says the confident adult. "You'll probably find someone better and never come back," comes the reply from within. Fortunately, as adults we can hear both messages and sort out rational fears from irrational ones. Perhaps we'll need a little extra reassurance on occasion. Basically, though, we can learn to accept that the people who love us want us in their lives—they will not abandon us, so we can feel safe.

Attachment and bonding is the core positive foundation of Belonging. Separation anxiety is the fundamental fear that gets activated when Belonging is threatened.

Parents nurture their children's need for Belonging. Above all, they show and tell their children that they are warmly appreciated: "You have a place right here. You will always belong with us. Welcome to the family." Children who get this message consistently throughout childhood usually grow up feeling confident that they are both loved and lovable.

Characteristics of Confident Belonging

The bonding and attachment skills learned as children help people become adults who are capable of Belonging with partners, families, and larger groups. These skills help people develop a capacity for confident Belonging, essential in incorporating Belonging into your life balance.

Inner Sense of Belonging

"Of course I belong." People with confident Belonging assume the best. They just feel that they are loved and lovable. Because they have experienced acceptance they don't worry a lot about rejection. That doesn't make them naive or pain free, though. They will hurt just like anyone else in the face of abandonment, betrayal, and loss.

Those with confident Belonging feel a fundamental security. They have a place in their family, a place in the community, a place in the world. They are not afraid of being left out of things. "I belong" makes sense to them. Their Belonging is part of them. In other words, they don't just have the potential or capacity to belong, they already belong. Just as the person with confident Being says "I am," with certainty, the person with confident Belonging says, "I belong."

Ability to Join

This deep inner confidence that comes from confident Belonging allows people to join gracefully with others. They seek connection. They expect friendship, partnership, collegiality, and love. They view bonding and union as something that can and will happen. Joining is satisfying.

People with confident Belonging realize that relationships take time, energy, and work. They also recognize that not all relationships work out. They're willing to take that risk, though, because they expect positive results. They're not paralyzed by the fear of rejection or abandonment. On the other hand, these people can say good-bye. They move away from others, firm in their belief that they can return. They neither cling to relationships nor flee from them.

One subtlety about the ability to join pertains to the quality of introversion and extroversion. Extroverts are people who are born with a desire to meet and greet others. They love contact. They like to talk, go places, and do things. Introverts are usually quieter. They are drawn towards a more inner life.

This doesn't mean that all extroverts have confident Belonging, though. Some extroverts lack confidence even though they connect quickly with others. They may fear and expect rejection. They may not quite feel they really belong, either. Sometimes, they sense that something is missing, perhaps real intimacy.

Nor do all introverts lack confident Belonging. Some do, of course, and that's one reason they stay holed up at home. But many introverts do have confident Belonging. They may be slow to connect. They may say little about themselves at first. They may seem to treasure their privacy and solitude more than relationships. Still, they value friendship and connection greatly. Life would be just as empty for them without relationships as it would for extroverts. Both introverts and extroverts may want and expect to have meaningful unions, just as they both are equally capable of having a lack of confident Belonging.

Strong Desire for Emotional Intimacy

Communication is like a pyramid. The base of the pyramid is by far the biggest area. That's where most communication takes place—small talk, the weather, grandchildren, etc. That pyramid base is important. It provides the structure for more important communications, such as sharing one's ideas, thoughts, hopes, and dreams.

Emotional intimacy exists at the very top of the pyramid. We are emotionally intimate when we share the deepest, most private parts of our beings. This is, "If you really knew me, would you still love me?" territory. Those with confident Belonging truly believe that others will like what they see when they reveal their real selves. Their disclosures will be matched by the other person. The result will be a trusting, caring, open, warm, and safe relationship.

But what if you try to share your real self and everything goes wrong? "Here I am, warts and all," you offer. "Ugh" is the response. Who wants scorn, disapproval, contempt, and rejection?

Those with confident Belonging will be hurt by this rejection, just like anyone else. They may have to pull away for awhile to lick their wounds. However, they won't give up on themselves. Ultimately they will conclude that the other person made a big mistake, not them: "Too bad they can't accept me for who I am, but that doesn't mean I'm a schmuck. I'll just have to find someone who will accept me."

One note here: not everyone in life wants emotional intimacy. For some people it's just too much bother. They'd rather be working or playing. They could be emotionally intimate if they worked at it, but they prefer not to. That's a choice each person must make. Hoever, one wonders if these people are cool to emotional intimacy because they are too involved in other things or because they've been scared or shamed away from closeness? Would they want intimacy if they could have it? If they were to gain more confident Belonging, would they then seek deeper relationships? These are questions only they can answer for themselves.

Loyalty

✧ Al is a friend's friend. One night, for instance, he saw that his buddy, Phil, was in trouble. Four guys had surrounded Phil and were about to attack. Al charged across the street bellowing something loud and awful. Those four thugs turned and ran. He probably saved Phil's life.

Afterwards, someone asked Al why he risked his own hide to help Phil when he didn't even know what the commotion was all about. "That's the way I was raised," Al answered. "You never let your friends down. You stick with them no matter what. Besides, Phil would do the same for me." ✧

You might argue with Al's judgment, but he is definately loyal. Loyalty is a trait of those with confident Belonging. That's because Belonging creates a strong sense of "us" and "we." People with confident Belonging have strong bonds with their families, friends, business colleagues, etc. "We're in this together," is far more than a figure of speech to them. It's real. They feel it. "We're going through life side by side, so we might as well hold hands."

There is such a thing as misguided or blind loyalty, of course. You're making a mistake when you are loyal to people who aren't loyal to you. Let's hope Al is right, though, when he says that Phil would defend him if their roles were reversed.

Appreciation of Similarities and Differences

✧ Marla, Louise, and Helen go back all the way to junior high. Now in their forties, they still get together a couple times a year. One day they went to a movie and shopping, laughing and talking all day. But when they went out to a late lunch, Marla began gently weeping at the back of a deserted restaurant while the others held her hands. She told them how her husband's drinking problem was ruining their marriage.

Louise could sure connect. She ended her first marriage because of her husband's drinking and gambling. The message that came through her warm hand into Marla's was, "I know what you're going through. I'm a lot like you."

Helen had never been through anything similar. In fact, she'd never married. But she was just as caring. Her message was more like, "We're very different, but I'm still here for you. Help me understand what you're feeling." ✧

Similarities and differences. People with confident Belonging respect both. They find common ground through their similarities. "We are a lot alike," is the foundation for many friendships and partnerships. However, they are also fascinated with the natural differences between people. They are curious about what others think and feel.

Gershen Kaufman often uses the phrase "interpersonal bridges" to explain how people connect with each other. These particular bridges take a long time to build. They are built not with steel but with understanding, caring, and interest in others. Interpersonal bridges span the gaps of human difference. They allow us to connect with each other despite our dissimilarities.

We discover "us" as we meet at the center of the bridge.

People with confident Belonging are good at building interpersonal bridges. They like the work. They're realists, though; they realize that bridges need repair and maintenance. Belonging takes continuing time and effort.

Good Boundaries

There's a fascinating paradox about Belonging. A strong sense of "us" is only possible among people who have a strong sense of "me." But a strong sense of "me" is only possible among people who have a strong sense of "us." The better I know me, the more I have to bring to us. The reverse is also true. The better I know us, the more I have to bring to me.

So the question is this: Is there something that simultaneously helps create a strong "me" and a strong "us?" The answer is yes. Good personal boundaries do both.

One Alcoholics Anonymous slogan is "stick with the winners." Now that's a strong boundary statement. The idea is to use your instincts, knowledge, and wisdom to let the good guys into your life and keep the bad ones out.

People can develop two boundary problems. They can have too thick boundaries. These keep everyone out, both good and bad. Or you can have too thin boundaries that let everybody in. People with confident Belonging have firm but flexible boundaries. Their boundaries let in the light but keep out the cold.

Ability to be Generous

✧ Clare, a thirty-year-old receptionist, has a definite dating philosophy. One of her basic principles is that she never dates stingy men. This isn't just about money, though. She believes that people who are stingy with money are stingy with their emotions, too. While Clare may be exaggerating and overgeneralizing, she has a point. Some people are more generous across the board than others with their time, energy, praise, and love as well as their money. ✧

People with confident Belonging are likely to be generous. Why? Because they feel connected with everybody, not just theirselves or their immediate family.

The formula is simple: people are usually most generous towards those they consider family, so the more people they think of as family the more generous they will be. Those with confident Belonging tend to have big "families," with which they share time, energy, and resources.

Sense of Communion

Communion is simply defined as any act of sharing. However, communion usually implies deep emotional or spiritual joining, a linkage of souls. People with confident Belonging often seek and find experiences of communion, making it possible for them to connect spiritually in many situations, not just within the context of organized religion.

Security in Relationships—A Combination of Being and Belonging

Good Belonging experiences, especially during childhood, lead people to expect more good Belonging experiences. People with confident Belonging grow up believing that others are basically kind and caring. At the same time, good Being experiences, especially during childhood, lead people to expect more positive Being experiences.

It takes both strengths to have consistently satisfying relationships. People with both confident Being and Belonging bring self-confidence and self-worth into their relationships; they also trust others. In other words, they have both a strong "me" and a strong "us." Their strong "me" keeps them from getting absorbed into the lives of their loved ones. Their strong "us" keeps them from becoming hopelessly self-centered.

People with confident Being and Belonging are a little like medieval castles with drawbridges; they have strong drawbridges that they can close whenever they want, but they keep their bridges lowered most of the time so that they can let the world in.

Challenges to Confident Belonging

We long to belong. Still, Belonging can be difficult. Sometimes our minds say "Yes, introduce yourself and start talking," while our bodies refuse to move forward and our mouths develop a serious case of glued lips. These blocks to Belonging can be weak, limited, and temporary. They can also be strong, generalized, and long lasting. Some of the most frequent challenges to confident Belonging are described in this section.

Fearing Abandonment

The fear of abandonment lies at the center of many Belonging problems. For babies, this fear is mostly physical. Infants sense their need for adults. They cannot survive on their own. They experience separation anxiety literally as the fear of death.

This survival fear gradually changes as the child grows. It becomes a new kind of fear. It is the fear of emotional starvation, which threatens whenever someone feels insecure in the area of Belonging. "I can't live without you," no longer means, "I will physically perish." Now it means, "I am nothing without you, I am emotionally destroyed."

Some people suffer more abandonment fear than others. Those with the most shame suffer the worst. That's because shame-bound people think of themselves as basically bad, useless, and unattractive. They truly believe nobody likes them, which really means they assume others dislike them as much as they dislike themselves. Nevertheless, almost everyone feels abandonment fear at least occasionally.

Now for the big question: What is the basic antidote for abandonment fear? What can help you feel more loved and wanted? Actually, there is an answer, and it is a deceptively simple one: Love and be loved. That is the only way to get rid of abandonment fear. Now let's break this answer into its two parts. First comes love, as in loving others. It's not all that difficult if you're not too scared. Besides, there's no other way. You've got to love others if you want to belong.

Too many people are afraid to love. They are too full of what-ifs: What if they won't love me back? What if they go away? What if they die? What-ifs do more harm than good. True, they protect you against the pain of lost love. But they do so by paralyzing you. What would you think about someone who is so worried about food poisoning that they totally refuse to eat? What's different about that than the person who is so afraid of abandonment they refuse to love? They're both going to starve.

Now for the other part—being loved. That, too, is a necessity for Belonging. Actually, the goal is to be open to love, since there are no guarantees that somebody will always be there to love you. Openness to love means actually hearing the caring in your partner's voice, accepting the comfort in your friend's hug, taking in the sincerity in your neighbor's interest, feeling the genuineness in your children's "I love you". Openness to love means letting go of another set of what-ifs. What if they're only pretending to care? What if they want to use me? What if they quit loving me? What if, what if, what if. The fear of abandonment is universal. However, that fear doesn't have to destroy or paralyze anyone. The urge to belong is stronger. Love and be loved.

Fearing Rejection

Good fences make good neighbors. But good fences can't be maintained when people are desperate. That's when the need to belong leads to serious errors in judgment.

✧ Take Willow. She's so afraid of being alone she'll do almost anything to keep a partner: "First, I grab any guy who so much as says "boo" to me. I don't care if he has the IQ of a dead horse as long as he's nice at the start. Then I do whatever he wants, including sex, so he won't leave me. All my friends tell me I've somehow found an even bigger loser than before. But I won't listen. I can't stand the thought of losing him. I get insanely jealous, too. The last time this happened I ended up smacking my boyfriend in the chest just because he glanced at another girl. They start thinking I'm crazy, of course, and then they do leave me." ✧

Willow makes four mistakes, all related to the fear of rejection. People who fear rejection often make the following errors:

- Rapid, unselective bonding. Grab them before they get away. It looks like love at first sight; it's actually an act of desperation. They're better than nothing, aren't they?

- Excessive compliance. Doing anything the other person wants in order to keep them.

- Inability to let go. "Maybe they're a bad choice, but they're all I've got." It's like hanging onto a balloon that's rising straight into the air. You're afraid to let go because you'll get hurt, but the longer you hold on the higher the balloon rises.

- Clinging dependency. "I can't live without you. I'm nothing without you. You are my entire life." You end up playing chase and run. You chase and they run. Your goal becomes never letting them out of your sight. Theirs becomes avoidance of intimacy and commitment.

The fear of rejection is different than the fear of abandonment. It's more active. With rejection fear, there's a nagging belief that, "I'm gonna mess up and that's why they'll leave me." By contrast, those who fear abandonment think that nothing they do really matters. They're going to be left aside and there's nothing they can do about it.

People who fear rejection must start believing more in themselves. They have to think of themselves as "keepers." Sure, they may make errors once in a while, but so does everybody. They need to discover a sense of safety inside them, too, so they don't rely on others to make them safe.

Getting Stuck in Independence

"I can do it myself!"

Seems to me I vaguely remember hearing this phrase when my kids were growing up—about a million times. "I can do it myself," is very important to the small child just beginning to master eating with a fork or tying their shoes. It's equally important to the teenager mentally preparing to eventually live on their own. "I can do it myself," is really about Doing, not Belonging. But that phrase often leads to another: "Go away!" That's where Belonging gets involved. Americans have been taught to treasure independence. Self-reliance is a virtue. Needing others is morally suspect.

◇ Here's an example. Teddy was about fourteen when he witnessed a strange and alarming scene. His father, very ill from cancer, was saying farewell to Hal, an old friend who came unannounced to visit. Hal slipped Teddy's dad a twenty-dollar bill in his parting handshake. Neither man said a thing. Teddy only noticed because his father looked a little embarrassed, his eyes lowered and his face flushed. The next day someone sent a fruit plate to the home. Once again Teddy's dad accepted the gift with lowered eyes.

Teddy understood. The family was out of money—a charity case. He felt deeply humiliated. What if his friends found out? Teddy felt disgusted with his father, ashamed of a man who needed others to survive.

Teddy never said anything. But the next day he applied for a paper delivery route. He personally vowed that he would never, never accept charity from anyone. Indeed, he would not let himself need anything, or anybody, again.

Once Teddy was a grown adult, he was fiercely independent, both financially and emotionally. "I won't accept charity," has generalized to, "I won't accept anything from anybody." The ban includes friendship and love because they could make him feel needy. Neediness in any form is totally unacceptable to Teddy. It smacks suspiciously of dependence to him, and dependence is to him shameful. Teddy is trapped in independence. He confuses dependence with closeness, intimacy, and love. ✧

People like Teddy are stuck because of a false dilemma. They think they have to choose between being cared for—dependence—and caring for themselves—independence. They also fear getting swallowed up by others if they ever let down their guard. This fear of engulfment is common among people who cling too tightly to their independence.

There is a way out of this false dilemma between dependence and independence. There is a third choice—interdependence. That's when people rely both upon themselves and each other. Interdependence is stronger than dependence, less rigid than independence. People who are interdependent know they can take care of themselves when they need to. However, they value cooperation. They look forward to times when they can work and play with others. Being on a team doesn't threaten their identities.

Teddy's life theme is "I don't need anybody." He's trapped on an island of his own making. He's totally self-reliant and totally alone. He's won his victory over dependence but the price is too high. Teddy's going to have to build a bridge to the mainland. The Interdependence Bridge allows two-way traffic.

Feeling Unloved and Unwanted

✧ Bruce thinks he's a reject. He's simply never felt good, good enough, or lovable. Might as well take him out to the dump and throw him away, as far as he's concerned. That would just save everybody else a lot of wasted time and effort.

How could this be? Who knows? Sure, Bruce has many memories of childhood rejection. His mother ignored him. His father favored his younger brother. His schoolmates wouldn't play with him. But which came first, Bruce's feelings of being unlovable or his memories of rejection? Maybe Bruce is forgetting the times his mother paid attention, his father took him to the ball game, and his friends came over to play.

Regardless, right now, Bruce feels unloved and unwanted, unlovable and unwantable. He feels Belonging shame. Bruce believes he is unworthy of relationship. As far as he's concerned, nobody could, should or ever would love him. Bruce lives an extremely isolated life. ✧

✧ Karen's problem with Belonging is a little different. She's been married to a wonderful man for four years. Still, she has her mental bags packed. Sooner or later, she just knows Vince is going to tell her to leave. She just can't believe their relationship is forever.

Karen's problem is doubt. She's not so shamed or damaged as to believe she's totally unlovable. But she worries. Vince might grow tired of her. He might find a more attractive woman. He might get sick of her for no reason at all. Her doubt is like T.S. Eliot's fog that creeps in on little cat's feet. Somehow it's there, sitting on her lap, when she least expects it. ✧

Can people heal their Belonging shame and doubt? Yes. But it takes time and effort. I recommend reading and counseling. Expect gradual change, with shame giving way to doubt, doubt giving way to confident Belonging.

Isolation

Isolation is the last big challenge to Belonging. There are at least four kinds: relationship avoidance, intimacy avoidance, community avoidance, and spiritual avoidance.

- Relationship avoidance. Some people actively avoid almost all relationships. They may do so from fear (social phobia) or from disinterest. They become loners, perhaps absorbed in their work. They often feel at least a twinge of loneliness, but they don't act much on those twinges, which after all, usually go away in a few hours or days.

- Intimacy avoidance. These people get involved in shallow relationships. They like to do things with people. They're often very active in sports, club activities, etc. They don't like to talk about feelings, though. In fact, "feelings stuff" makes them distinctly uncomfortable. "Can't we just quit talking and have a little fun?" is their life theme.

- Community avoidance. Very family oriented, these people seldom think much about the bigger picture. They don't take time for community activities. They may envy others who are more involved, but they make up excuses to avoid community contact.

- Spiritual avoidance. Here, people avoid deeper connections, the ones that help them feel they belong to something greaer than their limited selves. They decline to search for meaningful connections between themselves and the universe, sometimes only to feel a vague sense that something very important is missing in their lives.

Any act of avoidance produces isolation. Isolation, in turn, represents a limitation to Belonging. On the other hand, each of the four areas above is also an invitation. Each offers rich rewards to those who pursue them. Awareness of one's relationship avoidance leads to relationship contact. Similarly, awareness of one's avoidance of intimacy, community, and spiritual connection can lead to newfound treasures in these three areas.

Exercises to Help You Belong

Exercise—If You Really Knew Me . . .

Note the responses below that you most often think in response to this phrase: If you really knew me you would . . .

hate me

love me

accept me

reject me

be disgusted

be delighted

come closer

run away

_____

How comfortable are you with your responses? What could you do to change some of them if they are mostly negative and pessimistic?

Exercise—Who Would I Die For?

Take a minute to ask yourself a few loyalty questions:

1. Who would I fight for?
2. Who would I lose a job or promotion for?
3. Who would I die for?

Exercise—Moving Towards and Away

This exercise is designed to help you become more aware of your habits of distancing and connecting. It can be done with any two people. The less you know the other person, the more information you will gain about your general need for closeness and distance. The more you know the other person, the more specific information you'll receive about that particular relationship.

Here's what to do:

1. Stand at opposite ends of a room so that you are about ten feet apart.

2. One person (decide beforehand which one) then "calls" the other forward non-verbally, with gestures rather than words. The caller is in control. Stop the other person at just the point where you feel most comfortable. Any closer and you'd feel a little smothered. Any farther away and you'd feel too distant. Take a minute and both discuss your feelings.

3. With the caller still in charge, experiment by gesturing for the walker to come a little closer, and then farther, away. Discuss the results.

4. The walker returns to the starting point and now becomes the caller. Repeat everything.

5. In real life usually neither person is really in charge of relationship distance. After you've taken turns with the previous steps, try the exercise again, but this time both of you move forward, being both caller and walker. See if you can negotiate a mutually comfortable resting place.

Exercise—Reclaiming Your Right to Belong

Belonging shame and doubt must be challenged. If not, they'll go on and on, preventing you from feeling safe in your relationships.

Today is a perfect day for this challenge. Here's how:

1. Think of your Belonging shame and doubt as if it were a person. Specifically, as if it's an annoying person who's been tripping you up for too many years.

2. Write a letter to that person: "Dear shame," (or whatever label you choose). Put in the letter all the ways your Belonging shame and doubt have affected you over the years: the relationships you've blown, the ones you've been too afraid to begin, the ones you've been too scared to enjoy.

3. Now comes the most important part. Start a paragraph with these words (or ones like it in your own style): "I've decided it's time for you to go." Say why you need to do this. Write how your life will change ("From now on

I'm going to accept invitations to have coffee with people instead of making excuses," etc.).

4. Finish your letter with a firm good-bye. Read it several times to yourself. Read it to someone you trust. Keep your promises to yourself for your new behavior.

Exercise—Challenging Core Irrational Beliefs About Belonging

The goal here is to identify and challenge any irrational beliefs you have that limit your ability to belong.

The first step is to identify these irrational beliefs. Here are some examples:

- I'm unlovable.

- I can't love others.

- I'll never fit in anywhere.

- I'm different. That's why people dislike me.

- No matter what they say, they will always leave me.

- Don't trust anybody. They'll always betray you.

- I can't let go once I'm in a relationship.

- I should never need or depend upon anybody.

- I can't get close to others. Real intimacy is impossible for me.

- There's no place for me here. I'll always be an outsider.

- I always get left out of things.

- _____

Are any of these familiar? Can you think of others? Pay special attention to the one or two beliefs that most limit your ability to belong.

Take these beliefs one at a time. See if you can remember where they came from. When did you decide each core belief was true? Who told you so? What evidence did they have? Was their evidence accurate or false? True all the time or not? Were there exceptions that they failed to notice?

Know that these beliefs are irrational. They are overgeneralizations and exaggerations that unnecessarily limit your choices. They keep you from Belonging in ways you want.

Now choose the irrational belief that most limits your ability to belong. Try saying out loud the exact opposite belief. For instance, the exact opposite of "I can't get close to others. Real intimacy is impossible," is "I can get close to others. Real intimacy is possible." That phrase is no more irrational than the one you've believed about yourself.

Now find a middle ground, such as "I can get close to some people. Real intimacy is possible with them." How would your life change if you replaced your irrational belief with this more reasonable one?

Try living by this new, more rational belief for a week or two. See how changing this one belief affects your ability to belong. Then go back and challenge the next most limiting, irrational Belonging belief.

Exercise—Family Praise Circle

Nothing makes people feel better about themselves than praise. Children in particular thrive on praise. They grow emotionally with praise. They shrink with criticism. Indeed, one of the most reliable predictors of healthy families is the ratio of praise to criticism. The higher the ratio the healthier the family. But watch out for families in which praise is virtually absent while criticism is constant. That's where you'll find the meanest parents, the nastiest kids, and the biggest messes. Mutual praise promotes a sense of confident Belonging. Wouldn't you want to belong in a family that praises? And who wouldn't want to get out fast and forever from a family that only criticizes?

Here's an exercise for your family that helps everyone learn how to give and receive praise. First, gather up your family. Turn off the television and turn off the phone's ringer. Tell everybody it's time for a little family togetherness session. Get everybody to hold hands, unless such flagrant mushiness would spark an all-out rebellion.

You can begin the exercise by giving specific praise to one other person in the circle. The praise should be clear, specific, and honest. It may be about some positive quality of the receiver such as their intelligence or smile (Being). Or it may be about how they interact with others, such as "You make people feel so warm and welcome when they come to the house. You always seem to know how to put people at ease," (Belonging). Or it may be about something they have accomplished such as, "You sure did a good job on your homework assignment last night," (Doing).

The family member who receives the praise should take a moment to take it in. Tell them to "breathe in the praise," by looking at the praise giver, taking a deep breath, and saying thanks before going on.

The receiver now becomes the praise giver by choosing another family member to praise. Continue this routine until everybody has received at least two or three items of praise. Don't let anybody get left out but also don't force children to praise each other if they can't or won't. Parents, however, should never fail to praise their children.

Things to avoid during a praise circle:

1. False praise. This occurs when someone says something they think they should say but don't really mean.

2. Conditional praise. "I like it when you do the dishes . . . but you almost never do them." Praise followed by a "but" is really criticism in disguise.

3. Shrugging off praise. "Aw, it was nothing." Phooey on that. Take in the praise that's offered. It's meant for you.

So, does your family think this is the silliest thing they've ever done? That's okay. Just tell them you'll only do it a couple more times for practice. Meanwhile, see if the amount of praise doesn't go up in your household.

Exercise—Me, You, and Us

This is a simple exercise. It works for one person, but is even better if partners both try it. If you both try it, read the directions and then do your drawings separately, and don't compare notes during the exercise.

Begin by drawing two circles so that they overlap in the middle. Label the far left circle "me," the far right circle "you" and the middle section "us." Put all of your personal characteristics in the "me" circle. Words like crazy, fun loving, depressed, scared of life, or extrovert. Put your partner's (or ex-partner's, parent's, child's, etc.) characteristics on the "you" side. Serious, beautiful, troubled, insecure, down to earth, etc.

Now for the most important part. Name the characteristics of your "us." The "us" may have traits different from either of your individual natures. For example, adventurous, unstable, cuddly, insecure, or romantic.

Each "us" is unique. Each "us" brings out parts of you that might go unnoticed in other relationships. Each "us" is a product of the special connections between you and your partner. How do you feel about your "us"? Are there mostly positive or negative words there? What changes would you like to make? And how?

A sense of Belonging helps people feel safe, strong, and lively. Supported by others, you can more easily engage the world. But in order to do so successfully, people need to be comfortable within the sphere of Doing, the subject for chapter 4.

Chapter Four

Doing Is What Comes Naturally

Doing Brings Pleasure and Pride

✧ "I'm worried. All Marty does is sit around. He's not interested in anything anymore. Something's wrong with him. It's not natural just to sit around and do nothing, is it?" ✧

Good question. The answer is no, it's definitely not natural to do nothing. Actually, exactly the opposite is true. People have a powerful urge to do things and to get better at what they do.

A psychologist named Robert White began writing about what he called "effectance" back in the 1960s. White believed that humans have an inborn instinct to gain control over their environment. Mastery is the goal. Mastery is made possible by learning general skills such as reading and specific skills like how to quilt or change a tire. White suggested that people gain "primary pleasure" from these experiences. In other words, they enjoy becoming competent for its own sake, not just to put food in their bellies or money in the bank. It simply feels good to do things and do them well. White described a feeling of pleasure that comes from taking this kind of action. He called it the feeling of efficacy.

Researchers have followed up on White's powerful insight. He was right. People do strive for mastery. This push towards competence begins at birth. Think of how infants try to get their needs met. Each cry says something different, from "feed me" to "change me" to "I need a nap." Then think of a young child proudly showing off their ability to draw circles and squares and triangles. That child feels great about theirself because they are mastering a skill. "I can do it!" they say. The "it" is the skill in "I can do it." The "can do" is the process that brings pleasure. The result is an "I" who feels capable, energetic, and proud.

This chapter is about Doing. Action. Directed energy. Purpose. It is about pride and self-respect as well. It is about developing feelings of confidence and competence. The goal of Being is acceptance. The goal of Belonging is love. The goal of Doing is mastery, and its by-product is self-respect.

Children are instinctively motivated toward action and mastery. Parents can be very helpful, though. Here's a personal example:

✦   "Mom and Dad, guess what?. David just climbed up the stairs all by
    himself! I had to call you right away." We could hear the pride and
    excitement in our daughter Cindy's voice. She was thrilled that her
    nine-month-old son had done something new and challenging. First she
    congratulated him with kisses, hugs, and warm words. She let him feel her
    joy for him. She helped him know that he'd done something wonderful.
    Then she called in the family for a joint celebration.   ✦

Children thrive when their acts of Doing are encouraged. They love to hear words like "You've done it. You did it right. I'm proud of you." Children who get these messages end up feeling good about themselves. They develop a deep sense of competence, too. The child who gets praised today for climbing the stairs becomes the child who believes that, with appropriate effort, they can do whatever they want to do.

Parents are human. They sometimes make mistakes in the area of Doing. One common error is to discourage a child's initiative. "No, don't do that. You'll make a mess. It will take too long." Now, no parent has the time and patience to encourage everything a child wants to do. But "good enough" parents do encourage their children to try new things. They actively help their children develop a "can do" attitude towards life.

Overprotection is another mistake. Parents want to protect their children from trouble. However, their children's urges to explore expose them to danger. Overprotection is the all too easy result: "No, no, don't do that. You'll hurt yourself." True, children will get hurt as they explore, but the job of parents is to help their children grow, even if that means an occasional fall or wound. Parents must balance the need to protect with the need to help their children take responsibility for their own lives.

Some parents refrain from praising their children for Doing. They are afraid of spoiling their children, so they hold off. Or they demand perfection, forgetting that mastery is a slow process that includes many failures. Perhaps they don't appreciate their children's accomplishments because nobody appreciated theirs when they were kids. That's how low self-respect and self-confidence get passed from one generation to the next.

Finally, some parents too frequently praise their children for Doing. They want to build up their children's self-esteem, so they constantly tell them how wonderful they are. They forget to link praise with accomplishment. It's one thing to praise a child's scribble by saying something like, "Hey, that's good. I like that. Can you draw some more?" It's another to compare that scribble to Picasso. It's still another to imply to a child that they are so wonderful they don't even have to pick up the crayon and try to draw.

Doing brings pleasure to people of all ages. Directed action leads to feelings of mastery and self-respect. The overall positive sense that "I can do it" is often called competence or efficacy. I call it confident Doing.

Characteristics of Confident Doing

Having a Coping Response

✧ Belinda wasn't expecting her boss to offer the promotion; she'd only been working in the store for six months. But the old parts manager retired and her boss didn't think the other workers were very responsible.

Should she take it? It would mean a raise but also more duties. Belinda was a little scared. What if the job was too much for her? What if she failed? On the other hand, what if she succeeded? Wouldn't that be exciting! Belinda thought about it for a day and then accepted. After all, it was a challenge and she liked challenges. ✧

People with confident Doing have a coping response; basically, the coping response has two parts: accepting challenges rather than avoiding them and accepting failures as learning experiences that lead toward eventual success.

Accepting Challenges

Life is full of challenging situations like Belinda's: Should I ask someone for a date and risk rejection? Should I quit my job to go to school, even though I'm not sure what the job market will be like when I get out? Should I try to fix the plugged drain by myself or call for help? These situations are all alike. They're scary to try. You could lose something important if you fail (self-worth, security, time, money, etc.). But the rewards for success are great. Some people regularly accept these challenges. Why?

I think the answer lies in a story told by Stephen Lankton, a psychologist. Lankton tells a tale about a little boy and a dragon. That dragon lives on the edge of town. Everybody's afraid of it so nobody ever goes that way. One day, however, a little boy is late waking up for school. Still sleepy eyed, he stumbles towards that fire-breathing monster instead of away. Much to his surprise, the dragon grows smaller instead of larger. So the little boy walks even closer. The dragon gets smaller again. Finally he walks right up to that dragon, and guess what? It shrinks down so small the little boy can pick him up and put him in his pocket, which he does, taking him to school for show-and-tell.

The moral of the story? It's a lot easier and less scary to do something when you move towards it. It makes life more interesting, too. A good day becomes something more about challenge than staying safe. It becomes a day full of opportunities.

The opposite of the coping response is the avoidance response. Avoiders move away from psychologically risky challenges. The dragons in their lives are too large, too scary, too dangerous. Avoiders live their lives in unnecessary fear unless they take steps toward accepting the challenges life puts in their paths.

Treating Failures as Learning Experiences

✧ Marlon writes for a living. Several years ago, he submitted a book to several editors. They all promptly rejected it. His friend, Steve, offered him his sympathy, blaming "those nasty editors" for failing to appreciate him. Marlon stopped Steve, though. Marlon said he had reread his book and decided it was poorly done. He had managed to write a book exactly halfway between something meant for counselors and one for the general public. Those editors weren't being mean, they were just doing their job. Months later Marlon submitted two new books, one each for counselors and the general public. Both were immediately accepted for publication. ✧

Marlon learned from his failure. He kept going. That's the second part of the coping response. It's also a sign of confident Doing.

Treating Failures Like Speed Bumps

The message people with confident Doing tell themselves: "I don't like these bumps in the road. They really slow me down. But I know where I'm going and I'm not gonna let them stop me." The bumps delay them and make them think. Some of them can be painful, too, especially when they've been going too fast.

Avoiders, on the other hand, feel overwhelmed by any obstacles they encounter. Avoiders treat failures as stop signs. "This obstacle looks pretty huge. I don't think I can get over it. I might as well give up on ever getting anywhere." So they retreat back into their homes, or beds, or safe places. The trouble is they never get anywhere. Speed bumps are everywhere, after all. Treating them like stop signs guarantees failure.

Having Reality-Based Optimism

People with confident Doing tend to be optimists. When faced with a puzzle, they believe they have the skills and abilities to solve it. They enjoy a general sense of competence. Still, they are realists. Told to go out there and keep Michael Jordan from scoring, they'd probably not bet their homes on success. True, they believe in themselves, but they're not fools. But let's look at how a person with confident Doing tackles a more realistic challenge.

✧ Shelly was a good scorer in high school basketball, so she decided to try to make her college team. Here was her realistic but optimistic evaluation of the situation: I'm a good enough shot right now to make the team, but I never had to play much defense in high school, so I'm weak there. Luckily, I have all summer to practice.

Shelly accurately recognized her strengths and weaknesses. She also believed her weaknesses could be corrected with hard work. She signed up for a tough summer league and focused on defense instead of scoring. There were no guarantees of success, but she was determined to give it her best effort. ✧

Those with confident Doing believe in themselves for two reasons. First, they recognize the skills they've already developed in any specific area. Secondly, they trust that they can learn new skills and abilities as needed.

The feeling of confident Doing is like a camera with two lenses. One lens is broad. It reveals the big picture. When Shelly looked through it, she saw herself as a generally competent young woman who could pretty much do well at whatever she wanted to. The other lens is narrow. It focuses more clearly upon one area of life at a time, one domain such as basketball, social skills, money management, etc. When Shelly looked through this lens, for instance, she may have seen herself becoming a better shooter, passer, and rebounder. People with confident Doing use both lenses frequently. They look through the broad lens to gain a general feeling of optimistic confidence. Then they zoom in on the most important areas of their lives to become more competent.

Taking Responsibility For Your Life

Taking responsibility for your life is the single best predictor of positive change. Confident doers take responsibility for their own lives. They also refuse to take responsibility for other people's lives. They aren't "rescuers." They don't spend hours every day doing things for people who could be taking care of themselves.

✧ To illustrate the importance of taking responsibility for yourself, let me contrast two unhappy women, Trina and Penelope. Both are displeased with their relationships. Both live with partners with whom they experience definite communication problems. But that's where their similarity ends.

Trina is a blamer. She acts out the role of perpetual victim. "It's all his fault," is her favorite saying. She comes to therapy for only one reason: to find someone who will comfort her. Her counselor made the mistake of suggesting that she make some changes. "Why should I change?" she cried.

"It's not my fault." Then she started shopping for a new therapist, looking for someone who "understands" her better.

Penelope refuses to play victim. Sure, she also comes to therapy for understanding and comfort. But she's looking to change herself. The kind of questions she brings to counseling are these: "What can I do different that might help in my relationship? What can I do to help myself?" She wants and expects her therapist to challenge her a little. She knows that she is the only person who can really make herself feel better. ✧

Fortunately, everyone can build up their sense of confident Doing. All you have to do is take responsibility for your own life. The best place to start, of course, is in the areas you most want to blame others.

Having the Ability to Turn Wishes Into Wants

A wish is something that would be nice if it happened.

A want is something you're working on to make happen.

Random gambling (the kind where there is no skill involved, only luck) is big in Wisconsin. People lose hundreds of thousands of their hard-earned dollars on scratch cards, slot machines, and numbers pools. Why? Why do they go back again and again, throwing good money after bad? There are many reasons, of course, including chasing after action, simple enjoyment, and addiction. But there is another reason as well. It's the not-so-secret desire to get something for nothing. I call that desire "wish power."

Wish power. The idea that somehow, some way, you are going to get everything you want without earning it. You'll get lucky and then your worries will be over. This is not a component of confident Doing.

Confident doers do their share of wishing. They dream of owning their own homes, retiring early, finding their true love, raising families, being their own bosses, etc. But there is a big difference between them and these wishful gamblers. Confident doers take the time and energy to turn their wishes into wants.

How does a wish become a want? By choosing, planning, starting, following through, and completing. These are the five stages of Doing.

Confident doers are good choosers and planners. They think carefully about their options in life. Specifically, they decide which skills they most want to develop, how they will do that, and what they will do with those skills once they have mastered them. They are fairly realistic about what they can and cannot do, so they don't spend much time idly wishing for things they can never hope to accomplish. However, they are good at imagining themselves becoming more skillful. They can close their eyes and see themselves typing faster and faster, or learning how to switch car engines, or successfully investing in the stock market—after studying it for awhile. But note that they are envisioning a process, not just the final result. That's the big difference between wishers and wanters. Wishers only picture results, such as getting rich. Wanters picture themselves doing something—such as painting, selling, studying, or researching—that could produce those results.

Choosing and planning begin the process of converting wishes into wants. Starting, following through, and completing finish it; think of these three processes as different kinds of energy, each special and unlike the others. Starting calls for a quick burst of energy, much like a sprinter jumping off the line in a hundred-yard dash. Follow-through demands the patience and steady energy of a long-distance runner. Completing necessitates a final surge that gets you successfully to the finish line.

Each of these three areas can present problems. For instance, getting started is difficult for some people. You can't get what you want, though, without taking initiative. "Oh, I just haven't gotten around to it yet" is the graveyard of wants. Contrast that statement with "I'm working on it. It's going slow but at least I've got a start." What makes starting so difficult? For some people, there is a general block about taking initiative. For others, the problem is that their need for security overpowers their creativity. Still others may be failure oriented, hesitant to "waste" time on projects they think they will almost certainly fail.

Some people are great starters, but they still cannot convert their wishes into wants. That's because they have poor follow-through. They get bogged down in the middle of things. They get bored or distracted. Perhaps too many other things compete for their attention. Their lives consist of dozens of half-completed projects.

And then there are those who just cannot finish what they start. The person who flees their twenty-one-day treatment program on the twentieth day. The computer software specialist who keeps going back to the technical manual they're writing, never completely satisfied. The couple with fourteen home-improvement projects in the works who are still living in the basement of their self-built home. The person who cannot quite accept a divorce that occurred years ago and keeps hoping beyond hope to reconcile.

Some people are much better at one of these tasks than others. My wife, Pat, for example, is a great starter. If the two of us are offered an opportunity, she's begun it while I'm still at the, "Well, I don't know. Maybe we could do this, maybe not" stage. Her, "Come on, Ron, let's go. This will be fun," has got us into many wonderful doings that I probably would have turned down. On the other hand, I'm a good finisher. I like to close one deal before going on to another. I love the sense of satisfaction that comes when I can see the final product right in front of me. We make a good team. In general, the goal is to become proficient in all three stages of work: beginning, continuing, and completing. It's especially important to confront your weakest link; for example, relatively poor starters can master that art with practice and self-understanding. It's also smart to form teams that include different persons who are particularly good at each stage. That's one way to ensure that group projects will go well from start to finish.

Challenges to Confident Doing

People intuitively desire to do things and to do them well. However, the process is far from automatic. Much can go wrong, so that the coping response gives way to avoidance. Instead of moving towards challenge, people then move away, shirking opportunities as too dangerous. Certain of failing, they lose their confidence. Unconfident, they are unable to develop their skills. That lowers their self-esteem, producing a vicious spiral of avoidance followed by failure followed by more avoidance and more failure. Fortunately, though, this process can be reversed. It is possible to become more confident and competent, provided that the blocks to confident Doing are examined and challenged.

Having Shame about Doing

Shame is the main challenge to confident Doing. The primary message that comes with Doing shame is, "I'm not good enough." I'm not good enough to do things well. I'm not good enough to succeed. I'm not good enough to do anything right. Sometimes the shame is overwhelming. That's when people feel almost totally incompetent at everything they do. But often the shame is more subtle, leading to behaviors such as self-sabotage and perfectionism.

It is possible to heal Doing shame. First the shame must be examined and understood. But that is not enough. Then it must be challenged in action. Doing things differently and doing them better is what turns Doing shame into realistic pride.

Having a Sense of General Incompetence

✧ "I can't do anything right." So says Larry, a forty-year-old with many, many problems. Larry's drug addicted; he's so scared of people he won't even get out of the car when his girlfriend visits her family; he hasn't held a steady job in years; his only identified skill is organic gardening, but he can't make a living at that because of poor business abilities. Larry's biggest problem, though, is his absolute conviction that he is incompetent. He believes he is doomed to fail at *everything* he does, both now and in the future. ✧

✧ Karen's situation isn't nearly as extreme as Larry's. She's got a decent job. She's married and raising a family. Secretly, though, Karen has the same problem. She, too, believes she can't do anything right. Karen's quietly amazed at the end of every day that she hasn't been fired or divorced. She feels more like an actress playing a role than a real person doing life competently; Karen keeps waiting for someone to demand she get off the stage immediately. ✧

This general sense of incompetence almost always forms in childhood. It may be the result of obvious physical or verbal abuse. That's Larry's case. He grew up with brutal and violent parents who constantly told him he was both good for nothing and good at nothing. They sneered at his acts of Doing, whatever they were. They predicted Larry would fail miserably at school; so he did. They told Larry he would mess up everything he tries; so he has. Sometimes, though, you can't pin the blame on parents. Karen's an example.

✧ True, Karen's parents did push her to excel. Perhaps they expected a little too much. Maybe they gave too little praise. But Karen would be the first to admit she came from a normal family. She's always felt loved and accepted, too. "It's me, not them. It's just that I've never felt good about what I do." ✧

What can you do if you have a sense of general incompetence? The answer depends upon whether you are more like Larry or Karen. Larry needs long-term psychotherapy to help him emotionally separate from his parents and their doomsday prophecy. He needs to start life over. He'll probably need a combination of psychological help and specific skill-building training. Karen, on the other hand, needs to stay in the present. She must learn to challenge her perpetual competence doubts. Karen can do that by telling people when she feels incompetent (keeping her doubts secret makes them stronger). She'll have to learn to accept praise graciously. That means actually taking compliments in rather than just pretending to or shrugging them off. Most importantly, Karen needs to remind herself to look at the facts. The reality is she can do most things well. She needs to judge her competence by her actual record, not by her inaccurate "gut" instinct.

Having Feelings of Irrational Incompetence

"I don't get it. Normally I love a challenge but I shy away from computers. I just don't have confidence in that area." Computers. Plumbing. Math. Cooking. Sex. Sharing feelings. Religion. College. Athletics. The areas differ with each person, but the pattern is the same. People who have feelings of irrational incompetence erroneously believe they aren't good in a particular sphere, even though there is no support for that belief.

✧ Sali accurately evaluates her skills in most areas. Her overall sense of confident Doing is excellent—except for dancing. Sali told Wes that she was a terrible dancer. It took Wes over a year to get her out on the floor, and she caught on quickly. But at the end of the night she sighed and once again complained about her terrible dancing form.

Wes asked Sali why she thought she was such a terrible dancer, even after she danced quite well. Sali told him about her first big date at age sixteen. Her partner insisted they try a dance she didn't know. Sali literally fell twice to the floor. She still remembers the feeling of total embarrassment. Understandably, that's the moment Sali decided she was an awful dancer.

After some coaxing, Wes got Sali to agree to go out dancing more often, promising that she could always choose which dances they'd sit out. ✧

Ugly scenes like Sali's first date imprint themselves in your brain. They produce a deep sense of incompetence that ignores current reality. The brain says in effect: "Look, I suffered a terrible humiliation. I better avoid that area forever. I hate even thinking about it. The bottom line is I just can't do it." These locked-off areas of the brain float like islands of incompetence in one's sea of confident Doing.

It's not easy to sink these islands. They've been floating around for a long time. Still, they can be challenged and at least reduced in size. The key is to do what Sali did. Think about exactly when and how you decided you were inept in a particular area. Reexperience the scene. Share what happened—the actual event and your feelings and thoughts—with someone you trust. Then let go of the past. Reevaluate the situation based upon your current level of functioning. If you are actually pretty good at dancing, or whatever it is that you feel you're not good at, allow yourself to accept that fact. If you are not very good at that activity, but would like to be, remember that it may be simply because you've been avoiding that area for fear of reawakening your shame. You'll need to start over and practice.

Subjecting Yourself to Self-Sabotage

✧ Charelle is a talented artist. She's so good she could make a living through painting. She could, that is, except she hasn't finished a canvas in two years. She's begun a dozen, reached final stages with a few, but she cannot quite finish any. Charelle's pattern of self-sabotage began in childhood when she realized her parents seemed threatened by her successes. Long after she left them, though, she continued to fail in this peculiarly anticlimatic manner. ✧

Self-sabotage is any personal behavior that hampers, hurts, obstructs, or destroys progress towards your own goals. Examples include a teenager who completes their homework only to leave it in their locker day after day, a woman who saves for a house for years only to blow her savings on a foolish spending spree, and a man who loves his girlfriend but stalls so long about making a commitment that she eventually leaves him.

Self-sabotage is connected with the shame-based message, "I'm not good enough," but self-saboteurs actually have a fairly subtle version of this message. It's more like, "I'm almost, but not quite, good enough. That's why I fail just when it looks like I'm going to succeed."

Self-saboteurs tend to attract cheerleaders. They chant, "You can do it! You can do it!" only to become bitterly disappointed when the self-saboteur, once again, yanks defeat from the jaws of victory. They just can't understand how someone so talented can keep failing. The reason for the failure is that the self-saboteur is stuck.

People who sabotage themselves are caught in a conflict that rages inside them. On one hand there is the basic human urge toward action and competence. On the other is a powerful message to fail. The clever compromise is to almost, but not quite, succeed. That temporarily ends the conflict but settles nothing, and so the entire scene gets replayed endlessly. Self-sabotage becomes a lifestyle. The result is repeated frustration expressed in the form of a question: "Why do I keep messing up? Why does everything I do start out so well and then fail?"

Self-saboteurs must attack the "almost" in "I'm almost good enough." Who says or said "almost" to you? What feels right about the word almost? What feels wrong? What would happen if you dropped that word and let yourself be good enough? Then you need to study your self-defeating patterns, looking for ways to alter them. If Charelle usually stops painting at the point where she begins detail work, she'll need to challenge her rationalization that such work is boring or a waste of time. Most of all, she'll need to fight through the blockade so that she can experience feelings of mastery and completion. That's the only way to end the conflict between success and failure that immobilizes the self-saboteur.

Developing the Habit of Invisibility

❖ "Ma, look at me! I can ride my bike with no hands. Look!"
"Joanne, stop that. Quit showing off." ❖

Sound familiar? Joanne's mother is telling her it's not okay to let others see her ability. It's better to hide it so nobody else will feel bad or envious. Rather than being encouraged to become competent, she is encouraged to be invisible.

But competence doesn't grow in a vacuum. Becoming competent is a process. It takes time and effort. It takes encouragement. Skill building needs reinforcement, especially when somebody is just starting a new effort and experiencing a lot of frustration and failure. If, instead, a person's efforts are met with discouragement and disapproval, that competence may never be developed. "Don't show off what you can do," all too often becomes, "Don't do it." Joanne may very well quit riding her bike without her hands if nobody approves. She might even quit riding entirely, since it may no longer provide a challenge.

Joanne, like many people, is being presented with a false choice. She's told that she can either be good or daring. But why can't she be both? That's where the habit of invisibility comes in. The idea is to be competent but not let anybody know about it. This develops because the urge to do things and do them well is so strong. Some people don't quit in the face of disapproval—they go underground instead. Too many people are like Joanne. They hide their competence from others, afraid of rejection.

Distortions of Confident Doing

The next three challenges to confident Doing differ from the ones already discussed. Instead of lessening the urge to action, these three exaggerate it. They also distort the true meaning of Doing, so that the joys of Doing are lost.

Overdoing

"I am what I do."

✧ Max and Carol make a great partnership. They're both from hardworking families where the emphasis was upon productivity and success. Married for twenty-five years, they run an Italian restaurant. They each put in twelve-hour days at least six days a week. They value the idea of working side by side.

But lately Max has gotten a little restless. The restaurant is doing so well he knows he's not much needed there. Besides, he's wealthy enough to travel, something he's always wanted to do but never done. Unfortunately, Carol doesn't understand. "Max," she says, "There's still plenty to do around here. You could start a take-out service. You could take over finances. If you're bored just get busy." Carol simply cannot rest. She is what she does, so she would be nothing if she did nothing. Her entire identity is wrapped up in her work. Carol is an overdoer. ✧

Overdoers haven't achieved balance among Being, Belonging, and Doing. Instead, they do, do, do, letting Being and Belonging fade into inconsequence. They also have a very narrow definition of self-respect. They respect themselves only when they are working very hard. They feel shame, boredom, and anxiety when they aren't immediately doing something they consider useful. Overdoing can become compulsive. Work until you drop, take a few minutes to recover, and then work until you drop again. Overdoing is seductive. It feels so good to be active and productive that everything else gets ignored. Besides, there's always more work to do. Why stop now when you can have more, and more, and more of a good thing? Why stop when you are still getting plenty of "ah" feelings from Doing?

But all "ah" experiences turn into "ughs" if overdone. Think of a delicious cheesecake. The first piece is wonderful. The second not quite as good. The third is, well, filling. The fourth makes you sick. It's the same with Doing. Too much doing, unbalanced with Being and Belonging, is unhealthy. It sickens the soul. Overdoers need to learn to expand the meaning of their lives to include more Being and Belonging experiences.

Feeling Excessively Competitive and Focused on Comparison

Competition turns the art of Doing into the act of Doing better or worse than others. This can be stimulating and useful, but only if not overdone. Too much competitiveness turns your life into an unending contest.

✧ Brandon is a young man who says he's been "cursed" with athletic ability. Pushed by his ambitious father/coach, Brandon became a high school star in track and football. Along the way he became more and more demanding of himself. First place was the only goal that mattered. Second place was for losers.

Unfortunately, Brandon's career slowed after high school. He did get a college scholarship, but he simply wasn't talented enough to be a starter, much less a star. He dropped out after two years and returned home. Now in his late twenties, Brandon is nagged by his belief that he's a complete failure. He feels like he is nothing because he can't be first. ✧

Brandon's sense of failure is especially common in American society, because America practices comparative individualism. People are expected to rise to the top almost entirely by their own effort. The implication is that if someone succeeds than someone else must fail. Success is for "me," a "better me than you" event. There's little room for "us" in this way of thinking.

People like Brandon often develop two problems. First, they cannot turn off their competitiveness. Brandon's wife, for instance, won't let him play board games with their children because he has to win every time. Secondly, people who are excessively competitive cannot quit comparing themselves against others. The only question that matters is who is doing better or worse. Being "good enough" then becomes the same as being "better than." The natural desire to do and do well gets twisted into beating others out. That takes the satisfaction in doing away from the self.

Athletes have discovered two ways to guard against excessive competitiveness and comparison making. The first is to emphasize group unity, as in the old locker-room saying that there is no "I" in the word "team." This thought adds Belonging to Doing. It makes group success the standard, so that the entire team lives and dies together. There is still plenty of comparison making, of course. The competitiveness simply gets translated into "us against them" instead of "me against you." Still, the addition of Belonging does blunt the edge of comparative individualism.

The second alternative adds Being to Doing. The goal is to emphasize individual accomplishment instead of comparative achievement. This is the way of many long-distance runners whose main concern is racing against their own times. They may be running the Boston Marathon with thousands of other runners, but they are racing against themselves. Their personal achievements add meaning to their lives.

Note that these solutions don't take away a person's competitiveness. They add to it. People do best when Doing is balanced with Belonging and Being.

Needing Perfection

Being perfect = being human.
Making no mistakes = the only way to be acceptable.
Being imperfect = being worthless.

Do these three equations look a little off? They should, because none of them make much sense. Still, perfectionists believe them. They think they are only human and good enough when they are perfect. They think they are failures when imperfect.

Perfectionists are doers. But joy is missing in their Doing. That's because perfectionists are driven more by the fear of failure than the love of Doing something well. Their goal is to avoid making mistakes. Errors bring ridicule, shame, and self-reproach.

Perfectionists haven't accepted the idea that human beings are, by nature, flawed and prone to error. They confuse being good enough with being perfect, so that even small mistakes are devastating. That makes them never more than one step from total failure, no matter how well they've done.

Perfectionists try desperately to prevent any possible mistakes. They often become obsessive and compulsive, thinking all the time about possible problems and constantly checking to make sure nothing is going wrong. Life is dangerous. Life is hard. There's no room for joy, rest, or happiness when one moment of relaxation can bring disaster.

Here is one new equation, exactly the one perfectionists most need to adapt:

Being good enough = being human.

- What does good enough mean? Good enough means realizing that human beings are by nature flawed. It is useless for humans to try to become perfect.

- Good enough means knowing when to stop. Yes, sanding the desk is important, but it isn't wise to sand forever. The person who can't quit sanding the desk will eventually end up with nothing but a pile of dust.

- Good enough means finding the joy in Doing again instead of living in fear. It means setting positive goals rather than just trying to avoid mistakes.

- Good enough means accepting yourself as you are while simultaneously looking to gain wisdom and skill.

- Most of all, good enough means recognizing that your mission in this world is only to do more good than harm. We all make plenty of mistakes, but most of our mistakes can be corrected. The few that cannot be repaired usually teach us a great deal about our deepest wants, needs, and limitations. We do the best we can, and that's all we can do.

Exercises to Help You Do

Exercise—Naming Your Dragons

Dragons are the scary challenges that you've been avoiding for days, weeks, maybe years. Here are a few possibilities:

- That huge stack of paperwork on your desk
- The call to your possibly dissatisfied friend, client, associate, or relative
- The desire to quit smoking
- The need to really sit down and share your feelings and thoughts with your partner or friend
- The possibility that you've been walking down the wrong path for years but are too afraid to look for a new one
- The call from inside to develop a deeper and richer sense of spirituality

Can you name your dragons? What challenges have you been avoiding? Why? What do you want to do about them? What do you think would happen if you started walking towards those dragons, like the boy in the story did? Would they start shrinking? If they did, how would that affect you?

Exercise—Victims No Longer

Who have you blamed for your misfortunes? Your mother? Your father? Your childhood? Your God? Your partner? Your ex-partner? Your boss? Your children? Somebody else?

In what areas do you feel most victimized and helpless? Your self-esteem? Your capacity for intimacy? Your sense of safety or security? Your ability to work well? Your spirituality? Your financial situation? Your relationship with children or other family members? Your sexuality? Your health?

Pick one person and one area where you've been feeling particularly helpless and hopeless. Now ask yourself these questions:

- Am I ready to quit feeling like a victim with this person and this situation?
- If I am, how must I change my thinking?

- What must I do differently to go from being a victim to taking responsibility for my own life?

Exercise—The Feeling of Efficacy

Doing things and Doing them well brings a special feeling unlike any other. Perhaps you could use a reminder of just how wonderful that sense of accomplishment is. That's the purpose of this exercise.

Begin by going back in your mind to the last time you did something that you felt really good about. Maybe you built from scratch that shed you'd always wanted. Perhaps you spent an entire weekend with your children without screaming at them even once. Your special feelings may have come at work or play, alone or with others. You may or may not have gotten praise or approval from others, but the point is that you felt especially good about what you did.

Remember how your body felt as you went about that task. For some, the feeling is one of exhilaration and excitement. For others, it is more like peace and contentment. Go back to your thoughts. You probably were thinking ideas like "This is just what I want to do right now," and, "This is really important to me."

Remember the satisfaction you had just doing the work — not starting or finishing it but in the actual activity. This is the pleasure that is part of Doing. Above all, let yourself return to the joy you felt as you did what you did.

How long has it been since you've had that feeling? What can you do to have more of these experiences in the future?

Exercise—From Dreaming to Doing: Getting Practical

I spoke earlier about turning wishes into wants. The five steps to do that are choosing, planning, starting, following through, and finishing. Here are some important questions to ask yourself that will help you turn your wishes into wants.

Choosing

What are my deepest dreams, the ones that would bring me the most satisfaction if I could achieve them? What have I been putting off that I really want to do? What skills would I like to develop? If I could achieve mastery (meaning I'd get as good as

I possibly could) in any one area, which area would I choose? If I could begin today turning one of my dreams into reality, which dream would I pick?

Now choose one of your answers to use for the rest of these questions.

Planning

What specific goals can I set in this area? What would a camera record me actually doing? What is the first, most immediate step I need to take to begin moving towards my goal? What other steps will be necessary along the way? What specific barriers do I see between me and my goal? What do I need to do to overcome these barriers? What will my accomplishing this goal lead to in the future? What support (physical, emotional, financial, etc.) do I need from others to help me take this journey? What can I do if their support is limited, ambivalent, or nonexistent?

Starting

If not now, when?

Even though I can't know the outcome of this journey, do I still have the courage to take the first step? What can I tell myself to help me get started? What do I need to say to others as I begin this journey? What do I need to do? What do I need to think and feel?

Following Through

How can I maintain my interest and enthusiasm now that I've gotten started? What goals can I set along the way so that I can experience many small satisfactions? How can I realistically evaluate my progress? Where will I find the strength to keep going towards my goal despite the inevitable discouragements, frustrations, and failures I will encounter? How can I remember to enjoy the process instead of only focusing on the final result?

Finishing

How will I know when I have done enough? What is the last major step towards my goal? What do I need to do to take that last step? If completing things is hard for me, how will I sidestep that difficulty this time? What do I need to say, think, feel, and do to finish this particular project?

Doing is a critical aspect of life. With a strong sense of Doing, you are capable of accomplishing meaningful work. Without it, you may feel inept and unhappy. Doing alone, though, tends to be unsatisfying in the long run. The urge toward competent Doing needs to be integrated with desires for Being and Belonging if you are to achieve a balanced life. This integration is the subject for chapter 5.

Chapter Five

The Integration of Being, Belonging, and Doing

The Need to Integrate

Being, Belonging, and Doing are essential human needs. Each has its own origins and operates somewhat independently of the others. Any one area may be neglected or developed regardless of the others. Each may also be overdeveloped, by which I mean someone pays so much attention to that sphere that the others are ignored.

Nevertheless, these three forces are not completely independent. Think of Being, Belonging, and Doing as three streams that together create the river of life. The overall health of the river demands that all three streams flow smoothly and strongly. If any one of them is dammed or diverted, the river will flow that much more weakly. If all three are blocked, the river may be reduced to a trickle.

The three streams are separate. But once the waters intermingle it is impossible to tell them apart. That's why if you study any major event in your life you will undoubtedly have trouble neatly dividing it into pure vials of Being, Belonging, and Doing. Take, for example, something problematic such as getting laid off from work. That certainly is about Doing, of course, but it would probably affect your Belonging, since you won't spend time with your co-workers, as well as your basic Being, your sense of who you are. The same is true for more positive events like getting married. Tying the knot is a Belonging metaphor, but that decision involves seeing yourself as Being a different person and changing your Doing "lifestyle" as well.

Like the foundation, walls, and beams of a well-built home, Being, Belonging, and Doing naturally support each other. A house needs all three to be complete. It may fall apart if any of them has been poorly constructed.

I will describe three topics in this chapter. I will discuss the signs that one or more of these spheres is being neglected, the indicators that one area has been overdeveloped to the neglect of the others, and the cues that someone is actively integrating the three areas of Being, Belonging, and Doing into a complete whole.

Signs of Neglect

It's easier to tell that a house or car is being neglected than when someone is neglecting Being, Belonging, or Doing needs. The neglected house gradually produces many visible signs, such as peeling paint and cracks in the walls. But nobody goes around with billboards on their bodies saying, "I neglect Belonging." The indicators are far more subtle. Besides, most of the damage to people occurs on the inside, where it may be invisible both to observers and to the people themselves. There are regular cues, though, that one or more areas are being unattended.

Disinterest

One sign of neglect is simple disinterest. Lack of curiosity.

✧ Scott neglects Belonging by turning down repeated opportunities to meet others, not because he is too busy with other things, but because, "Well, to be honest, I'm not very interested in people. I'd rather stay home and watch TV than go out for the evening." ✧

Sheila ignores her Being needs because she can't be bothered with that "self-aware-ness stuff." Similarly, Penny can't imagine finding pleasure in work and so never thinks about her possible calling, failing to notice her Doing needs.

Negative Identity

Those who neglect an area often have a negative identity in that sphere. "That's just not me. I'm not the kind of person who thinks a lot about myself"; "I've never been good with people. I can't imagine that changing"; "I'm a thinker, not a doer." They are not be-ers, belongers, or doers, and not being those things is a big part of how they see themselves. Challenged to move beyond these self-imposed limitations, they often have difficulty even visualizing themselves as active participants in the missing realm. To become a doer, a belonger, or a be-er would mean they'd have to revise their entire sense of self.

Dismissal or Prohibition

Sometimes an area may be actively dismissed or prohibited. Here, one or more of these needs has become tainted with shame or guilt. It becomes something bad, something to be avoided, a target of scorn.

✧ When someone suggested therapy to John, he replied, "Taking time to find out who I am by seeing a counselor? No way! That would be an ego trip, a sure sign of selfishness and immorality. Only a raging narcissist would waste time and money on that therapy crap. I've got more important things to do." ✧

John feels terrible when he does anything for himself. He was taught that he's only good when he takes care of others.

✧ So what's wrong with Belonging? "Nothing," says Denise, "if you are weak and need others to hold your hand every time life gets a little tough. I value my independence; I rely upon myself and only myself." ✧

✧ "Doing?" Pat says. "Anybody can do things. What's so special about that? My Dad always told me the smart thing to do was to get others to do the work. He told me only fools have to get off their duffs. The smarter you are, the less you should have to do anything." ✧

These people have disowned their yearning for either Being, Belonging, or Doing. To want those things is bad, weak, dumb, evil. Chances are, those needs were invalidated by important people when they were young. The result is an irrational but powerful prohibition, a, "thou shalt not be ... or belong ... or do," that greatly hinders their lives. These prohibitions must be challenged with new thoughts and actions. "I have the right to be ... and belong ... and do. I will never give away that right again."

Missing Something

The people who neglect or reject an area may have a vague sense that they are missing something. It's hard for them to even put into words exactly what is absent. They feel confused, unable to say what is bothering them. Nevertheless, they sense that their lives would be richer and more complete if they could only take more time for self-reflection or connection or doing what they really want. But these nebulous wishes never become wants. The neglected sphere remains a low priority that never rises to the top of the pile.

Anxious, Unconfident, and Incompetent

Those who've neglected an area may also feel anxious, unconfident, and incompetent when offered opportunities to develop in those regions. They feel relatively inept in that sphere, unable to relax or to enjoy the experience. That leads to avoidance, poor follow-through, and failure.

Signs of Overdevelopment

Being, Belonging, and Doing are powerful natural forces. Like the gravity of stars, each pulls people steadily towards it. Furthermore, the pull seems to increase the closer you get. Normally, the attraction of each is balanced out by the others, so that every person develops their own complicated orbit. But sometimes the gravitational force of one sphere seems to overpower the others. Instead of a shining beacon, it acts more like a black hole. When that happens, the person is swept in closer and closer until it seems that escape is impossible. Eventually their world becomes one-dimensional. Only Being, or Belonging, or Doing is allowed.

Just as there are signs of neglect, so are there signs that one area has become overdeveloped at the expense of the others. However, these signs may be seen better by others than by the people in the black holes. These individuals may feel quite alive and invigorated, completely unaware that they are missing anything at all, but they may feel bored and disinterested when pulled away from that sphere, even temporarily. Thus, the hard-working farmer agrees only reluctantly to come in from the fields to be with his family. Once inside his home, he promptly falls asleep, not from exhaustion but from sheer disinterest in anything not called work.

Another sign of overdevelopment is that most of the person's identity and self-worth becomes associated with only one area. In addition, overspecialized people may believe that the only way to gain approval from others, or to avoid disapproval, is through one area. "I'm a dreamer," says the expert on Being. "Family is all that counts," claims the belonger. "I'm always busy," says the doer. Each has a clear but limited identity. Furthermore, those who've overspecialized have a narrow focus for self-worth. They feel pride only in tightly defined areas. Try, for example, telling a belonger that he is quite aware of his own needs or that he is very competent at work. Expect a shrug that means, "Fine, but that's not important. What I really want to hear is that people like me and want me around. That's all that matters." Disinterested in anything else, they often decline invitations to explore the other arenas of life. This choice makes them more and more dependent upon their one specialization for energy and self-esteem.

Overspecialization produces two obsessive-compulsive tendencies. The first is a sense of anxiety when threatened by a loss of involvement in the overdeveloped sphere. Told that he must take a week off for vacation, for instance, the overdoer begins to worry. "What will I do for a whole week if I can't go to the office?" Scared, he solves the problem by conjuring up excuses to call in every day and to bring work along on his holiday.

The second obsessive-compulsive trait is an inability to cut back in an area, even when trying to do so. That's when Being, Belonging, or Doing become psychological prisons. The overuser of Being becomes so self-absorbed that they cannot force themselves to attend to others. The overspecialized belonger loses their sense of identity, their "me," and instead can only think in terms of "us." Asked to focus upon themselves, they try to do so but cannot keep that frame of mind for more than a minute. Soon they drift back into the world of "us" and "we" without even hearing the change. The overdoer, meanwhile, tries to take a break from work and action but becomes so anxious that they cannot sit still. They know intellectually that there is more to life than Doing, but they cannot resist the pull toward action.

Overuse of any one arena produces habits of thinking, feeling, and action. These habits direct the person toward that sphere and away from others. One's life narrows in this process.

Measures of Integration

Here is a list of the major ways you can act to balance your Being, Belonging, and Doing needs. Integration is enhanced by:

- Setting a goal of balance: both daily and long term. This includes maintaining conscious awareness of the need to develop each area.

- Declining the temptation to overdevelop one area at the expense of the others.

- Seeking life patterns that maximize all three areas by adopting a "both/and" instead of an "either/or" model of how the three needs interact.

- Listening for the voice of each area.

- Developing individualized metaphors that interweave the three into an emerging whole.

- Promoting growth in each area over time.

Setting a Goal of Balance

It is important to strive for balance—both daily and long term, maintaining conscious awareness of the need to develop each area. You can't build a solid house without a floor plan, no matter how good your intuition. While the roots of Being, Belonging, and Doing are instinctive, still they cannot be fully developed without a conscious plan. Lacking an overall design, it's just too easy for one or another of the spheres to get neglected in the press of daily activity.

Integrating Being, Belonging, and Doing starts, then, by setting the goal of balancing these three forces in your life. But that goal can be broken down into two parts—your life plan and your daily activities. With regard to life plan, it's important to ask yourself what your life would be like five, ten, or twenty years from now if you achieve balance among these areas. Daily life, though, is more specific. What will today be like if you make sure to include aspects of Being, Belonging, and Doing? How about tomorrow?

Integrating these three needs demands conscious choice. That can only happen when you become fully aware of the need to nurture Being, Belonging, and Doing in your life.

Declining the Temptation to Overdevelop

Several years ago my twin brother, Don, said something in passing that had a tremendous impact upon me. He mentioned that he was feeling good because he had developed the ability to say "no" to good opportunities. He explained that his career was taking off and he had many offers to lead workshops and give talks. At first he had accepted them all, but in doing so discovered that he was neglecting personal and family needs. So then he became more selective.

Sometimes it is necessary to say "no" in one sphere in order to say "yes" to the others. That is especially true when one area is being strongly rewarded or when there is extreme pressure from others only to do one thing ("You're such a good mother. Why would you want to go to school?").

Overspecialization is the result of saying "yes" too often in one area while neglecting the others. Usually the overspecialized person will correctly feel that something important is missing, sensing at least vaguely that there could be more to life than narcissistic self-study, spending all your time connecting with others, or single-mindedly staying busy.

Seeking Maximizing Life Patterns

Just as the organs in our bodies usually function harmoniously, so do the three forces of Being, Belonging, and Doing normally support each other. True, conflict is possible, much like those occasions when a person's defense mechanisms inadvertently attack and weaken the body's own immune system. But this kind of conflict is rare, indicating serious problems in the system.

People who believe that there will or must be conflict among the three needs are thinking in "either/or" terms. Either I can have a "me" or an "us." Either I can have a family or a career. Either I can work hard or take the time to meditate. Thinking like that guarantees tension between the three areas. It creates many agonizing choices, many of which really don't have to be made.

By adapting a "both/and" model it is possible to seek life patterns that simultaneously develop all three areas. The question isn't any longer, "which of the two or three must I choose between," it becomes, "how can I live a life in which I maximize all three areas? How can I have a "me" and an "us" that support each other? How can I develop my career in such a way that my family is included? How can I utilize meditation to help me work more effectively? A "both/and" model eliminates many apparent conflicts. On the other hand, it sets a higher standard. It's not enough to choose an activity that enhances one area. That activity must at least not diminish the other spheres and should enhance them as well.

The acid test for any choice becomes this: Does this activity promote all three areas in my life? If not, is there any way to alter the activity to improve my total life?

Listening for the Voice of Each Area

There would be no reason to read this book if Being, Belonging, and Doing always spoke with firm, clear voices. "You need a week entirely for yourself. Schedule your vacation immediately and tell your family you're heading to the cabin alone"; "You will find someone to love and make a commitment by the end of March. No excuses"; "Listen here, pal, you better get off your duff today and find something meaningful to do with your life. I mean now!"

That's not how they work, though. The forces that propel these needs are often subtle. More often than not, Being, Belonging, and Doing speak softly. Sometimes they only whisper or hint at their existence. For example, becoming a little bored with your life as it is may signal a desire to attend to Being, while daydreaming about the last family reunion may tell you that you need to make time for Belonging. "Just browsing" through the employment section of the newspaper even though you like the job you have may be a signal to look at your Doing concerns. Furthermore, their voices can be drowned out in many ways. None of them can compete with a blaring television set, for instance, nor with an addiction or even loud arguments. They are gentle and persistent, however, like an ocean breeze on a quiet day. Turn off the television for awhile, refrain from drinking or drugging, stop screaming at each other, and there they are. Those voices have been patiently waiting for you to notice them.

There are several ways people can train themselves to hear these voices better. Journaling. Meditating. Therapy. Prayer. Alone time. Relaxation and breathing to lessen the screams of anxiety. Talking with friends or just thinking about Being, Belonging, and Doing. The common theme is that each of these routines takes time and commitment. Each method shuts out distractions because people just can't hear the voices of Being, Belonging, and Doing while distracted. The more you listen for the voices of Being, Belonging, and Doing, the more you will hear them.

Interweaving the Three into an Emerging Whole

I liked playing baseball when I was a kid. The trouble was, I grew up in a poor neighborhood where there was an equipment shortage. One boy would own a ball, another a bat, a third a glove. We had to get everybody together to have a good game. We also had to keep conflict to a minimum. Who wanted the game to end with somebody marching home with the bat?

That scene could serve as a metaphor for how Being, Belonging, and Doing interact. Three necessary ingredients: bat, ball, and glove. The need to bring them together in order to put them to best use. The emerging game is much more interesting and enjoyable because all three elements are there. The need to cooperate or face the possible loss not only of one piece of equipment but of the entire game.

Playing ball is a metaphor that has an emotional impact for me. For you, though, it may have none. So here is a list of several more metaphors for the integration of Being, Belonging, and Doing:

- A talented trio consisting of soprano, tenor, and alto. Each has solo parts. Together, though, their voices blend and enrich each other. Their harmony warms and completes you.

- You are gathering together three fabrics. One is coarse, red, vibrant. The second is smooth, yellow, calming. The third is textured, green, pastel. Imagine weaving these three cloths together into a colorful and everchanging design.

- Three paths through a darkened forest, converging at an opening where sunlight pours through.

- Three balls, each different from the others, all thrown into the air and caught by you, the juggler.

- Three streams, merging to make a strong river that takes you all the way to the sea. You want to fully explore each stream as well as the emerging river.

- You are building a house, needing a strong foundation and solid walls and beams, each useless without the others but together creating a safe and worthy structure. Once built, that house keeps you safe and warm.

The idea is to find a metaphor that has personal meaning, one that can truly serve as a vehicle for your growth in the areas of Being, Belonging, and Doing. Then you can check back with your image whenever you wish, using it like a compass on a walk through unfamiliar woods. Am I going in the right direction? How does this action fit into my metaphor?

Promoting Growth in Each Area over Time

Being, Belonging, and Doing are strong forces. Like an abandoned apple orchard, they can survive untended for decades. True, the apples from those deserted trees may be small and rusty, but they are edible.

People sometimes rediscover their abandoned orchards. Delighted, they fertilize, prune, and tend those trees. Sure enough, next fall the apples are bigger, juicier, and disease free. Rejoicing, they feast on their well-deserved bounty. But then they go away. They think that they'll have good apples forever. If not, they believe they'll always be able to return and fix the orchard again. Their interest wanes and off they wander, perhaps in search of new and better trees.

Soon, of course, the apples get small and wormy. Worse, the trees may start to die, especially if they are left to survive major droughts or cold spells on their own. Busy with other things, though, their owners might not even notice the problem. Or when they do they may have forgotten the directions to the grove so that they have difficulty finding their way back. Even so, however, they sense they must return to the orchard. Only there can they experience a real feeling of peace and serenity.

Being, Belonging, and Doing need regular tending over your entire lifetime. Only then will your orchard produce its finest fruit.

Exercises to Help You Integrate

Exercise—Challenging the Neglect of One of the Areas

There are several indicators of neglect mentioned in this chapter: disinterest in any one of the areas; negative identity development; active dismissal or prohibition of having any needs in that sphere; a vague sense of missing something important; and feeling anxious, unconfident, or incompetent in one area. The question here is how you may continue to neglect an area once you have become aware of it. This is done mostly by giving yourself messages to continue the neglect process. Common messages are ones like "I don't have time for Being (or Belonging or Doing)"; "I'll never be any good at it, so why bother?"; "I'm too scared / weak / vulnerable / sick / neurotic to try"; "I'll begin as soon as . . . (the weather turns warm, my divorce is final, I finish this project, etc.)."

What excuses, justifications, and rationalizations do you use to maintain your neglect of your least attended area? What could you say or do that would break through your self-neglect?

Are you ready to make a commitment, *today,* to focus more time and energy upon your most neglected area? If so, what specifically are you going to do to help you with this personal promise? Make a list of these promises, and keep it in a place where you will see it regularly.

Exercise—Challenging Overdevelopment of Any Area

Signs of overdevelopment include: disinterest in other areas, inability to cut back in the overdeveloped sphere, fear and anxiety when the overspecialized area must be left for awhile, personal identity totally involved in one sphere.

What messages do you give yourself that encourage overdevelopment of one area? Some common messages are, "I'm only good at one thing so I better keep doing it";

"I'm addicted to Being (or Belonging or Doing) and I can't help it"; "I like Belonging (or Being or Doing) so much I have no need for the others"; "I'm can't try something else. I'll never succeed."

Now think of a counter message that will challenge your assumptions. Perhaps, "I'll get better at other things once I take the time to practice them," or, "I can use my compulsivity to try out another area" or "I may be scared but I won't let that stop me." Does that message have any emotional power for you? If not, keep looking for one that does. If your message does have power, use it to help you make and keep a commitment to relax your hold on your overdeveloped sphere so that you can more fully explore the others.

Exercise—Create Your Own Personal Story

Create a story in which you, the protagonist, successfully turn from someone who has neglected or overdeveloped certain life spheres into a more fully functioning person: "Once upon a time there was a stubborn young woman named _____ who only rode bicycles. Never ever would she walk. Nor would she ride in a car. "Bicycles are for me, and nothing else," she'd say again and again. But one day _____ received an invitation to visit a country far, far away, across the ocean. She thought and thought about that invitation, trying to figure out how to get there on her bicycle. When she finally realized she'd have to get off her bike she said . . .

The integration of Being, Belonging, and Doing helps you develop breadth as you explore the many areas of living that make life interesting. But exploration of these three areas also assists in the ongoing search for spiritual depth, that which gives deep meaning to your existence. This subject will be discussed in the following chapter.

Chapter Six

The Spirituality of Being, Belonging, and Doing

Seeking the Intimate and the Infinite

Being, Belonging, and Doing are essential human needs. They direct our daily thoughts, feelings, and actions. Still, most people seek more, yearning to make deeper connections with the universe. The religiously oriented seek meaning in organized religion, with rituals of church services, prayer, and fellowship with others of the same religion. The nonreligious seek their own forms of truth and meaning. Here, spirituality is defined as the concern for the great mysteries of life that transcend our immediate interests.

Lately, particular emphasis has been placed upon "soul" as well as spirit. Soul is the actual embodiment of spirit in the human body. The concept of soul brings spirituality into daily life. Soul is body; spirit is mind. Soul is particular; spirit is general. Soul is intimate; spirit is infinite. Soul is the sacred ground above which spirit soars.

Being, Belonging, and Doing speak to soul and spirit. To soul, they offer immediate hope and direction. Can you find a deeper meaning or purpose in yourself, in others, in your actions? If so, you are discovering the most intimate connection between yourself and the universe. To spirit,

Being, Belonging, and Doing offer long-term guidance, a road to the infinite. What gives your life its greatest meaning? How can you join and merge with all that surrounds you? What work might fill you with a sense of mission and goodness?

Spiritual Vitality: The Spirituality of Being

The word "spirit" is derived from the Latin word meaning "to breathe." In Genesis, the Judeo-Christian story of creation, God breathes life into Adam, thus beginning humanity. Adam is filled with air, energy, vitality. He lives. He is. Adam is aware of his existence and of the presence of something greater than himself.

Spiritual vitality defines the connection between Being and spirit. Spiritual vitality is a way of breathing. As you must inhale oxygen in order to exist, you must inhale the universe in order to be spiritual. You take in the universe and become filled with life, energy, and strength. You are invigorated. There is "that of the Universe" within. The mystery of the Universe is still unsolvable, of course, since no one can see the entirety of a picture while still part of it. However, the mystery now resides within. Your bodily existence is an integral part of the great unknown.

Spiritual vitality means sensing yourself as a sacred part of a sacred Universe. Since every breath is sacred, so too is your body and mind. The focus upon Being allows you to find the spiritual within yourself, built into every motion and deed. This kind of spirituality is beyond judgment. It isn't that only certain acts are spiritual or that you can only sense the presence of the Universe in your good thoughts and deeds; the Universe is in every breath you take. It is within.

Still, there is responsibility. You must become aware of your sacredness, not in a narcissistic belief that you are particularly special (after all, everybody else is breathing in the Universe, too) but with awe and a sense of wonder. You need a humble gratitude to appreciate the sanctity of each breath and to appreciate the great gift of life. As Thomas Moore discusses in *Care of the Soul*, we need to feel our existence, not to overcome life's struggles and anxieties, but to know life firsthand, to exist fully in context.

The remainder of this chapter consists of a series of questions that may help you think about your particular spiritual relationship to Being, Belonging, and Doing. You may have quite clear answers to some of the questions, while others will take considerable pondering. Hopefully, these questions will serve to guide you gently toward increased self-understanding and self-acceptance.

What about your existence fills you with curiosity, wonder, and awe?
Curiosity is the desire to know. The power of curiosity involves wanting more information. What about yourself do you want to know more about? Your early years? Lost memories? Your unconscious? How long you will live? How well?

Wonder is astonishment or surprise. More than simple curiosity, to wonder recognizes the mystery of Being. What about your life amazes you? That you exist at all? That somehow you are alive at the turn of the twenty-first century? That you can walk and talk and think and plan and hope? That you can love?

Awe is a word that originally meant feeling dread and terror. Now awe can mean something internal, a bittersweet mixture of fear and reverence. Awe adds a sense of personal responsibility to self-awareness. To feel awe about your own Being is to recognize your power and to take responsibility for every choice you make. For instance, physically strong people may fear their own power. Consequently, they may vow never to use their strength carelessly, accepting responsibility for the use or misuse of their gift.

What about your life brings about this feeling of awe? Your physical strength? Your ability to understand other people's feelings? Your creative talents? Your sexuality? Your aggression? Your love? What strengths, skills, and powers do you have that you fear?

Curiosity, wonder, and awe are aspects of spiritual vitality. We become robots without them, passionlessly performing our life tasks. With them, we constantly expand our appreciation and interest in that part of the sacred residing within.

What about your Being can you least accept? What would it mean to accept yourself entirely? One aspect of spiritual vitality is to learn to accept ourselves as we are. Since the sacred dwells within our Being, how can we reject anything there?

But self-acceptance is difficult. It's easy to feel ashamed of your shortcomings and guilty about your lusts. Wanting to be perfect mirrors of the goodness in the universe, people constantly search for flaws in their images. Then they try to scratch them out, sometimes damaging their mirror even more in the process.

✧ Jamie, for instance, can love almost anybody because she looks for their assets and accepts their flaws. She is a kind-hearted and generous teacher who sees the good in all her students, even those like ten-year-old Rod, who is defiant of authority and aggressive to other children. She senses Rod's underlying strengths and does all she can to help him feel better about himself. Jamie's basic message to others is that they are fundamentally good. She feels their sacredness, the beauty of their Being.

Sadly, Jamie finds one exception to this general rule that all are sacred—herself. She is the one person whom she can't allow into the circle of universal goodness. Full of shame and doubt, Jamie cannot sense her own worthiness. She always finds reasons to believe she is not "good enough." She cannot accept herself entirely. If only Jamie could realize that she, too, is sacred. Jamie breathes in the universal spirit like all others. Perhaps, then, she could be as kind and accepting of herself as she is of others. ✧

There is a principle in Gestalt theory sometimes called the Paradoxical Theory of Change. This theory can be stated very simply: We cannot change anything about ourselves until we first accept it. The first step of Alcoholics Anonymous illustrates: "We admitted we were powerless over alcohol—that our lives had become unmanageable." The paradox is that some alcoholics who accept being powerless somehow find the strength and support to quit drinking. They change themselves only after accepting themselves as they are, not as they'd like to be.

The Paradoxical Theory of Change is about acceptance. First, you accept. Then, perhaps, you change. Often, however, change isn't needed once you accept yourself as you are. The woman who accepts her dislike of children may decide once and for all not to force herself into parentage. The man who realizes he's more sociable than aggressive willingly gives up his wish to become a leader. He had thought he'd be a failure if he didn't advance from member to leader, but then he realized he'd have been a failure if he had.

What does it mean to accept yourself entirely? It means to feel your essential goodness, a goodness that exists alongside your flaws, weaknesses, and vulnerabilities. It means breathing in the Universe without apology.

How can you accept your human flaws while still feeling the sacred within you?

✧ Dean is a Lutheran minister deeply committed to helping people with their spiritual issues. Unfortunately, he himself often struggles with deep feelings of personal insecurity. At the spiritual level, he feels unworthy to take in the love of the Universe.

Dean uses a visual metaphor to describe his situation. He imagines that his soul is a cup into which all the people who love him try to pour their caring. Unfortunately, Dean's cup is broken. The caring drains out through numerous cracks, chips, and holes. Each flaw in the cup represents one of his weaknesses, such as envy, anger, and despair. ✧

Dean's cup is broken, but he's not alone. Whose cup of life hasn't been damaged over the years? Nobody is walking around with a perfect vessel, free from the wear and tear of everyday life. Dean thinks his problem is that his cup alone is broken. In reality, we are all in some way broken cups, with chips, indentations, and holes. The question is not, "Is my cup intact or broken?" Instead, it is, "Can my cup be full of holes and still be holy?"

Will you let yourself feel within the presence of something greater than yourself no matter how damaged your personal cup of life? Can you feel sacredness within you, in everything you do, in all that you are? Do you feel the spiritual within you in every flaw as well as in your strength and beauty? This feeling of compassionate self-acceptance is part of coming to know your Being at the deepest level of love and respect.

When do you feel most alive and vital? What gives your life its deepest meaning? Inhaling the universe is a natural antidepressant. It fills us with life, energy, vigor, and vitality. But how can we stay attuned to that life force in our daily routines?

The key is to notice what most invigorates you. That might be working out in the weight room, raising a child, selling encyclopedias, writing short stories, or practicing religion. Whatever it is, that particular activity produces a special feeling. Somehow it feels just right. That activity fills both your mind and heart. You feel renewed instead of exhausted, as if you are drinking the purest water from a clear pool in the forest.

Existentialists like Irving Yalom say that the only way to find meaning in life is to throw yourself into it. You don't find meaning by studying life or disengaging from life. You find meaning by jumping in. The two questions at the beginning of this section are really one. Whatever helps someone feel alive and vital also gives life special meaning. Spiritual vitality is the result of this dual process.

There is a flip side to this discussion. People easily become depressed when they cannot find these pools in the forest.

They complain that life is dull. They feel like they're going through the motions without energy or joy. They may keep wandering through the woods for awhile, but they know they're missing something important. Their lives seem to be purposeless, without meaning. If you feel this way, perhaps you most need to stop what you're doing so you can rest and dream. Most of all, you need to ask yourself this question: what can I do that will help me feel alive and invigorated?

How are you dealing with the inevitability of your death? These are three ways to face death: with curiosity about the unknown, with resistance, or with acceptance. Each is powerful in its own way, with its own beauty and reason. Each has its place in life. One way to approach death is with a sense of curiosity, wonder, and awe described earlier. Only now it applies to dying as well as living. This sense of wonder allows people to break through the denial that keeps them from even thinking about death.

> *There was a young man dying from AIDS several years ago who embodied this curiosity. He wasn't terribly religious so he was uncertain of his future. He was neither afraid nor unafraid, but he was curious. His last words were, "This should be interesting."*

We may also face death with resistance. As living creatures, we are endowed with an instinctive will to live. This life force is incredibly strong. Our bodies insist on continuing, sometimes even against the conscious will of their owners.

> *Death with Dignity?*
> *No Way!*
> *They're gonna have to drag me out of here kicking and screaming.*

Then comes acceptance. Die we must. Somehow we have to prepare for death. If not we will live in terror of the inevitable.

> *Charles Whitfield asks this question: "Regarding your death, are you prepared and unafraid?"*

People use all three ways to consider death throughout their lives. Sometimes resistance is needed, sometimes acceptance, sometimes curiosity. All three may occur simultaneously, as with a person fighting cancer who reads about death while going through chemotherapy and writing their will.

As thinking human beings, we are fully aware that being implies nonbeing. Yes, we will die. Oddly enough, spiritual vitality is increased when we address that reality. Facing death helps people commit to life.

Intimacy, Grace, and Communion: The Spirituality of Belonging

Ira Progoff, the founder of the Intensive Journal process, uses a wonderful metaphor to illuminate the spiritual aspects of Belonging. Imagine yourself, he says, as the water in a single well, rising steadily to the surface. That water represents your individual life. Periodically, though, you feel a need to travel down the well so that your waters can merge into the common pool. It is there, in the depths of shared communion, that you renew your spirit. You then return to your separate well, to your private life, letting the waters rise. You may need to make this spiritual odyssey many times, returning on each occasion transformed and more intimately connected with the universe.

Spirituality is an intimate event. But intimacy is a strange word. It refers both to that which is most private, the characteristics of our deepest nature, and to sharing those aspects of the self with others. An intimate relationship, then, is one in which we disclose our most private selves to others, trusting and hoping they will accept us as we are.

True intimacy is spiritual. It occurs whenever people share their most private, vulnerable aspects with others, and when others do the same with them. This kind of revealing transforms the self. A person is never quite the same after having shared that deeply of one's self with another.

Spiritual intimacy occurs when you see and feel sacredness in something outside of yourself. That something may be a person, a tree, the wind, the sun, the galaxy, the universe. Whatever it is, it becomes sacred. Spiritual intimacy involves complete acceptance of that which is outside yourself. The world is not something to alter. People are not meant to be changed. Spiritual intimacy accepts that which is as that which is exactly right.

We are all capable of these exquisite experiences. But, being mere humans, we are incapable of staying there. We judge, we control, we attempt to change everyone and everything about us. But then we feel an interior tug, a pull towards intimacy. If we respond we rediscover the divinity of everyone and everything around us. If we fail to heed that tug, we feel terribly alone because judgment is invariably isolating.

Spiritual intimacy simply means to experience the greatness of everything around us, to be humbled by the majesty of the universe. There is a more specific concept, however, that links spiritual Belonging with a more traditional Judeo-Christian concept of God. The name of that concept is "grace."

Grace is the idea that God accepts and forgives people no matter who they are or what they've done. The state of grace is not earned; it is not about one's doings. It is about feeling a deep sense of Belonging with God. As Lewis Smedes remarks, grace is a sense that God accepts you, holds you, affirms you, and would never let go of you, "even if he was not too impressed with what he had on his hands." Smedes believes that being accepted is the most compelling need of our lives. But humans are incapable of total acceptance of others. Only God can accept someone with no possibility of rejection. Grace is the feeling a person has when they feel God's complete and unconditional acceptance.

Belonging is a healing experience. By feeling deeply loved by another, whether by God or another person, we feel less shame and more love for ourselves. Accepting others without judgment, we also judge ourselves less. Ultimately, we gain a sense of communion, the feeling that we are emotionally connected and committed to each other as whole people. We become part of a whole, an "us" that brings fulfillment, meaning, and a sense of completion. The "us" may be as small as a couple, two people linked by a bridge of respect and caring. Or it may be enormous, connecting someone with the universal past, present, and future.

Spiritually connected in this way, we feel the intimate in the infinite.

Here are some questions, and comments upon the questions, that help link Belonging with spirituality.

When do you sense sacredness in others? What about others fills you with curiosity, wonder, and awe? It's too easy to become self-absorbed. Fortunately, the world is so powerful that sometimes the sacred comes to us. Glancing up from the computer, you spot a beautiful sunset that makes you take a deep breath. Your daughter sneaks up and hugs you from behind just when you most needed comfort. You are filled with wonder and gratitude. How did she know? You hear that a friend died suddenly and you're flooded with memories of the times you spent together.

But that's not enough. As powerful as those moments are, they occur despite us rather than because of us. Frankly, most people have to work consciously to sense the divinity in others. We have to put our critical natures on the shelf so we can see the goodness in others. We have to quit thinking about how we can use people for our purposes and start thinking about how we can celebrate their existence. It takes conscious effort and discipline to stay focused upon that which is sacred in others.

When do you allow yourself to see the sacred in others? How do you do that? When do you let yourself be curious, full of wonder and awe?

How can you deal with your abandonments, betrayals, rejections, deaths, and losses and still maintain an openness to connection?

"I love you and I'll never leave you."

Yeah, yeah. Sure. But maybe that's what your dad said before he abandoned the family. Or what your partner said before they had that affair. Or what your friend said before dying in an auto accident. Why should you trust anyone again? After all, they could leave you too, no matter what they promise.

Some badly hurt people play it safe by avoiding deep commitments. Others become suspicious, questioning their partner's every move and thought, searching for clues they will be abandoned. Still others get desperate, overprotecting the people they love. But these aren't very effective solutions. The first leads to emptiness and isolation, the second to paranoia, the third to endless anxiety.

The spirituality of Belonging must deal with loss. That's because love is bittersweet. Just as life implies death, Belonging implies loneliness. There is always the possibility of loss today, the certainty of separation through death later. There are basically two ways that people can deal with their losses from a spiritual perspective. First, some people handle their losses, especially death, through religious faith. They believe the circle will be unbroken when they reunite in heaven or in their next life, for example, with those they've lost. Faith heals their wounds and helps them carry on despite their grief. They may not understand the grand plan, but they feel comfort abiding by it.

The second way to deal with loss depends upon a different kind of faith, namely faith in the intrinsic goodness of humankind. The core idea is that people are born with a natural capacity to bond. People instinctively seek closeness, intimacy, love. Yes, we all mess up occasionally, shooting ourselves in the foot by hurting the people we love. Sometimes we even reload and shoot the other foot. But basically people are inclined to care for and love each other.

There's plenty of love to go around. There's more than enough for each of us. To receive our share, though, we need faith in others. To give our share we need faith in ourselves.

What is the greater meaning or message in your loneliness? Loneliness is a messenger. It always has something important to tell us.

The trouble is that the message can be a painful one. That's why many people flee from their loneliness. They run to alcohol, sex, bad relationships, work, or frantic play. They run as fast as they can but somehow become even more lonely. And still the messenger keeps knocking at the door.

Here are a few of the most powerful messages your loneliness may be trying to deliver:

- You need to find someone to love

- You need to make a commitment

- You need to become your own best friend

- You need to attend to your family

- You need to stop ignoring your Belonging needs

- You need to grieve your losses

- There's something missing in your relationship(s) that you can no longer ignore

- You need real friends with whom you can share your deepest thoughts and feelings

These bittersweet messages will guide you when you have the courage to listen to them. They will help you find your innermost self and steer you towards satisfying relationships.

How are you most deeply disconnected from others? From nature? From the universe? From forces greater than yourself? What are the roots of your separation? You blew it. You weren't there for me. Go away. I hate you.

There is a central heartache, a burning complaint, a bitterness within everyone. That complaint reflects our deepest unmet Belonging needs. It is the inevitable result of human imperfection. No matter how well we are loved, our parents and other loved ones cannot always be there for us in exactly the right way at exactly the right time.

Disappointments are never minor in our unconscious minds. Each and every one of them gets stored as "proof" that others can't be trusted. Feeling neglected, we store up our pain, waiting for an excuse to lash out. "You're a terrible Mom," my friend's daughter told her recently, "You've abused me all my life." Pressed for examples, the daughter railed about her mother's failure to bake her enough chocolate chip cookies. Apparently baking cookies equals being loved in her mind, so not enough cookies meant not enough love. But no mom can bake enough chocolate chip cookies for their children. Nor can a partner always remember to say, "I love you," a boss always praise the good work of a subordinate, a partner always remember to enter the checks they wrote in the joint checkbook.

These disappointments spawn a sense of spiritual disconnection, causing people to feel set apart, unable to love or believe they are loved. They can become mean spirited, crawling into their caves and shoveling dirt across the opening.

So here's the problem. The universal complaint is, "Why weren't/aren't you always there for me?" The universal answer is, "Because I can't be." That is the root of human disconnection and the source of an ongoing spiritual Belonging crisis.

Somehow we must find a way to accept this reality. We must be able to accept our friends' and lovers' inevitable failures, even the universe's apparent neglect (Recently an eighty-two-year-old woman in snow-plagued southern Minnesota said she had prayed to God to let just one weekend go by without snowing, but that He must have been too busy to hear her). But what can you say to yourself that will help heal this pain? I love you despite your shortcomings? I love you because of your imperfection? Your saying will be unique. But whatever it is, the healing statement you say to yourself must maximize connection and minimize self-pity.

Here are a few examples of healing statements and the persons who designed them:

✧ "They've done the best they could, considering how they were raised." From a woman who cut herself off from her parents because of their shaming and blaming behaviors. ✧

✧ "I realized I've been demanding more from her than I could ever give." From a boyfriend who thought he needed his girlfriend's constant attention. ✧

✧ "It's time for me to quit shaking my fist at God." From a young widow whose husband was killed in a preventable industrial accident. ✧

Spiritual disconnection is inevitable. The challenge is to reconnect through accepting the world as it is.

When and how do you let yourself feel most deeply connected with others? With nature? With the universe? With God? One day my wife Pat and I were strolling, hand in hand, around a pond. The sunset was beautiful and I said something like, "Isn't that beautiful?" She agreed, we hugged, we continued on. Later I told her how marvelous I felt sharing that sunset with her. "What sunset?" she asked. Pat had been appreciating the beauty of a swan. Well, I'm a looker upper and she's a looker downer. But so what? We still shared an incredible moment. We both felt a special sense of Belonging.

Such moments never just happen. We prepare for them. We get ready by dumping our mental distractions. Forget about work for a moment. Let go of the past and the present. Leash our ambitions to a post, next to our fears, knowing full well they won't stray. Those fears and ambitions will be right there, more than ready for us upon our return, probably waiting to get fed so they can keep growing. But in the meantime we can have moments of spiritual connection, intimacy, union, and Belonging.

There's no need to reinvent the wheel here. Almost everyone has felt a deep sense of Belonging. Each of us knows how to belong, although we may need a refresher course if we've been disconnected for too long. If that's you, begin by asking yourself when you felt most deeply connected with others, the universe, and nature. What did you do then to help you feel Belonging? Perhaps you regularly called your sister. Maybe you went to worship services more. Possibly you asked people out on dates, for friendship or romance. Or you took every Saturday off just to be with others. Chances are good that you could do more of the same again, now, and that it would still work. You can also look for new opportunities to belong, such as joining a personal growth group, a sewing circle, a prayer group, a book club, or by taking a class or going to events to be around others with similar interests.

Belonging is a choice. How often do you make it?

Finding Your Calling: The Spirituality of Doing

Not all activities are created equal. Some fill people with joy, satisfaction, and spirit. One goal in life is to discover which activities are special to you and then to take part in them.

⟡ Mary has found a unique activity that gives her life extra meaning. She's founded a charity that takes in stray and discarded animals. She spends many hours every day feeding these dogs and cats, finding them homes, and fighting for more humane animal treatment. Helping those animals, almost all of whom would be dead without her, adds a special joy to Mary's life. For Mary, this charity is her calling. ⟡

A calling is a strong inner impulse toward a particular course of action, possibly accompanied by conviction of divine influence. This includes a sense that certain activities are particularly meaningful to the self and valuable to the world.

The concept of one's "calling" has changed over the years. When Max Weber wrote his famous book, *The Protestant Ethic and the Spirit of Capitalism*, at the turn of the twentieth century, he described a calling in terms of duty. A person's calling was a task set by God, a life activity in which someone fulfilled their earthly obligation to God. Personal satisfaction was not a goal.

Now a calling is more personal. It comes from within, filling a person with positive feelings. Truly good work is exciting, challenging, comforting, and fulfilling. It stirs the imagination and helps you grow. By finding your calling, you feel affirmed from inside. Your inner voice says, "Yes, this is right. This is what I most want to do with my life." Sometimes the speaker adds the belief that their calling "is meant to be," although meant to be by whom is usually left open. There is also often a feeling that some greater good will come from following one's calling, something that will benefit not just the doer but others as well.

A calling, then, is partly about Being because a person who finds a calling feels more real and alive. It is also about Belonging, since the good that is done goes beyond personal gain. Above all, though, a calling is about Doing, because it is a response to the question, "What do I most want to do with my life?"

The idea of a calling adds many spiritual elements to Doing. Callings emerge from deep within the psyche, give meaning to life, help people transcend immediate self-interest to seek a greater good, and connect people with the universe. They are inherently mysterious as well. Nobody can exactly explain why one set of tasks feels like a job while another is a calling, especially since one person's work may be another's calling. Raising a child is a calling to one father, a chore for another. Building cars may be just a job for one person, but what another person feels they were meant to do.

Doing, however, is not just about finding the "big picture" in your life; the deepest aspects of Doing are not entirely about finding one's calling. Doing is about soul as well as spirit. If seeking your calling is spirit, then noticing your daily actions and choices is soul. Mending the fence post, buying groceries, house cleaning, changing the baby. All these daily activities can be joyful and satisfying. They help people feel connected with themselves, each other, and the universe. Indeed, for some persons, the soul aspects of Doing are more important than finding a calling. What matters most to them is that their daily activities reflect their core values.

Here are some questions and comments about Doing and spirituality.

✧ *Which of your day-to-day activities are filled with spirituality? Which are dispirited?* Georgia is a magical baker. No matter how busy she gets, she conjures up her favorite breads and pastries several times a week. Then she brings them to the office where they are heartily consumed by her exceedingly grateful colleagues. But Georgia isn't baking just for the accolades. She simply loves the sticky, smooth feel of dough in her hands, the wonderful scents emanating from the oven, the crisp crusted texture of the finished loaves, the delicious taste of fine baked goods.

Georgia is filled with spirit when she bakes. She feels alive and energized. Furthermore, baking feels right for her. It's part of her life plan, her destiny. Take her away from her baking and a special part of her life would be missing. Georgia might quit her job tomorrow if she won the lottery, but she'd never stop baking.

There is a flip side to this conversation. Some activities can be dispiriting. If so, they seem to drain energy out of you. Georgia, for instance, gets no satisfaction at all from sewing, her mother's favorite pastime. Sure, she can count those cross stitches, but to her it's just a bother. Spending time sewing is intrinsically boring to Georgia, no matter how much she'd like to please her mother. ✧

Is it possible to feel joy and satisfaction in every single activity you do? Probabaly not. Too much of every person's life is composed of responsibilities and routines.

It's important to notice which of your daily behaviors really fill you with spirit. It's even more important to practice those activities.

Does your work fill you with something more than personal pride? The reward for spiritually centered Doing goes beyond money, prestige, and power. It is even more powerful than ego satisfaction, since we can do many things that provide an ego rush but don't feel particularly spiritual. Rather, spiritually centered Doing feels profoundly meaningful. There is a strong sense that the activity is intrinsically valuable and that it connects us with the universe.

This is a difficult concept to grasp in highly competitive America, where it is taught that the goal of work is personal success, usually measured by one's salary. Not much effort is made to help people find out what activities would really be important to them. One result of this is that many doctors, dentists, executives, etc., make a lot of money but feel deeply disturbed by the lack of joy their jobs bring them.

Locked in by their incomes, they fear listening to their inner voices. What if that voice told them to look for another line of work? How could they sacrifice all that money, prestige, and power? What would people think of them?

There is another approach, though, to finding meaningful work, which is to find the spiritual meaning in whatever you do. The bored doctor might find their work fascinating again if only they could feel the spiritual significance of their work.

Before quitting any activity, it is worth asking yourself if the problem is in the job or in yourself. Is it the work or the worker that makes an activity spiritually significant? Chances are for most people that both are true. Yes, some kinds of work offer more spiritual opportunity for a particular person than others, and it is possible to find spiritual meaning in everything we do.

One other factor is important when discussing the spirituality of Doing: the atmosphere of the workplace itself. Thomas Moore asks several questions about work and workplace that shed light on this issue:

- What is the spirit here?

- Will I be treated as a person?

- Is there a feeling of community?

- Do people love their work?

- Is what we are doing and producing worthy of my commitment and long hours?

- Are there moral problems in this job or workplace?

Workplace conditions do matter. When morale is high, most workers feel that what they're doing is meaningful and significant. On the other hand, it's hard to feel spiritual about Doing when the work lacks personal meaning, when the workplace is segmented or unsupportive, or when your co-workers attitudes are primarily negative.

What is the "mission statement" of your life? A few years ago my colleagues and I hired a business consultant to help our counseling center survive in this era of managed care and health management organizations. The first thing he asked was to see our mission statement.

Good idea. The problem was that we didn't have one. We just did what we did, we said. That wasn't enough, he said. He wanted us to really think about our core values and beliefs. What was it that we most wanted to accomplish? He insisted that we develop a short, clear statement that we could all agree upon. It could not be so vague that it meant nothing ("To do good in this world"), nor could it be too detailed and program specific ("To run three anger management programs a week, two aftercare groups, etc."). Rather, it had to describe our most important agreed upon values and our ideas about how to implement them.

It's not just organizations that need mission statements. So do individuals. Each of us can write personal, spiritually oriented mission statements. Such statements have two main parts:

1. Important core values and beliefs that you want to live by

2. A general sense of how you intend to carry out that mission

Here are examples of several short mission statements:

"Above all, I want to live honestly and responsibly. To do so, I promise to speak the truth whenever I can, even when I am afraid to do so. I will also hold myself accountable for my actions. I won't blame others, duck responsibility, or expect others

to rescue me. I will face the truth about my own behavior and improve it myself when necessary."

"I want to treat the world with respect. I want to honor the natural beauty and order on this planet. When I die I hope to leave the earth in slightly better condition than before. Some of the things I can do to respect the world are to use as little fossil energy as possible, to reclaim spent resources, to refrain from eating other living creatures, and to actively promote planetary awareness at home and work."

"When I evaluate everything I believe in, it boils down to one phrase: I want to be caring and compassionate in everything I do. For me that means I must refrain from cross words since angry language creates an angry spirit. I must take the time to really hear others, both what they say and what they cannot say. I must freely express my love to my partner and children and remember how much I care for them even when things go wrong. I will try always to look for the goodness in others and to respond to others with kindness."

"The most important goal in my life is to serve God. I know that means different things to different people, but to me it means above all putting personal gain and self-interest aside and doing things that serve the community. That's why I contribute my time and energy to several charities and why I declined a job with a company that had a reputation for abusing people. I also need to spend time in daily prayer and meditation, asking for guidance and direction."

There are many possible core values that could be part of someone's personal mission statement. Some of them are honesty, respect, responsibility, compassion, courage, justice, fairness, equality, democracy, sobriety, moderation, stoicism, generosity, kindness, appreciation of diversity, and self-reliance.

An Exercise to Help You Determine Your Core Values

Exercise—Writing Your Mission Statement

Take some time now to write your own mission statement. Select from the list of core values above or use values of your own. If you are having trouble selecting from several, here is the acid test: ask yourself which of any pair you would select if you had to choose between them. For example, if you were in a situation in which you could be either honest or kind, but not both, which would you pick?

Another way to discover your core values is to ask yourself how you would feel if the epitaph on your gravestone mentioned only that value: "A person of courage," "A compassionate person," "A generous person." Would you be satisfied? If not, what would have to be added or changed?

Once you've selected one or two main values, then go on to the second part of your mission statement. How can you implement those values into your daily life? For instance, a person who decided that generosity was their core value began a practice of starting each morning with a vow to be generous that day with their time, energy, and money. Then at night they reviewed their day, looking for evidence of generosity. When they found it, they felt at peace. When they didn't, they renewed their promise without beating up on themself. What can you do to actually live by your core values?

Write out a one-paragraph mission statement. Share it with someone you trust. Keep it with you. Review it from time to time and be prepared to rewrite your mission statement as necessary. One last note. Mission statements are guides, not punishments. Yours should feel good to you. It should feel right.

It should feel like an invitation, not an obligation.

The spiritual quest is a very personal and private manner. However you carry out that quest, though, your willingness to address the issues of Being, Belonging, and Doing will help illuminate your path.

The concepts of Being, Belonging, and Doing apply to every major aspect of human existence. Soul and spirit is one of these arenas. Emotion is another. As you will see in the next chapter, each of your central emotions can be divided into Being, Belonging, and Doing components and given a distinct name.

Chapter Seven

The Being, Belonging, and Doing of Emotions

The Role of Emotions

Emotions are temporary departures from calmness. They tell us that something is important. Emotions force us to pay close attention to the world. They amplify and magnify any particular situation. Emotions put muscle behind all of our wants, drives, and needs. They make us really want to meet that person, really care who wins the ball game, really love our children.

Emotions do the same for Being, Belonging, and Doing. They make them important. Emotions are closely connected with Doing because they act as guidelines to action. Without them, nothing would feel especially right to do. Should I go to school? Should I get married? Should I take the day off? Without emotion, the answer to all of these questions would be "Who cares?" With emotion, you care a lot.

What about emotions and Belonging? Emotions add the ache of loneliness to the fact of Being alone. They add tears of love to the fact of Being together. Emotions turn the desire to belong from theory, "Gee, it might be nice to find someone," into fact, "I'm not gonna sit here alone another night. Who can I call?"

Then there is the relationship between emotions and Being. Emotions are the difference between "I exist ..." and "I exist!" Emotions allow us to celebrate our Being. They may also drive people to the brink of despair, even to suicide.

Every feeling has a Being, Belonging, and Doing component, and it is useful to give these parts names. Here are some examples for some of our most basic emotional states.

States of Emotional Being, Belonging, and Doing

Emotion	Being State	Belonging State	Doing State
Joy	blissful	loving attached intimate	engrossed
Shame	defective	exposed rejected	weak inadequate ineffective
Anger	self-hatred	betrayal	frustration
Fear	mortal terror	separation anxiety	paralysis
Sadness	melancholy despair	sorrow grief	bereaved languishing

Joy: Blissful, Loving, Engrossed

Joy is a positive emotional state ranging in intensity from mild happiness and contentment to extreme ecstasy and euphoria. It is a temporary state like all emotions. Nobody is continuously joyful. The function of joy is to signal to people that whatever they are doing is very good and should be continued now or repeated later.

The Being part of joy is bliss. As discussed earlier, bliss means "complete happiness." Bliss happens when someone is joyfully involved in present experience and free from anxiety, guilt, obligation, judgment, doubt, obsession, and distraction. Bliss is a state of inner contentment that validates the self. Bliss occurs when people feel the power of the simple statement, "I am."

Several words help describe the Belonging state of joy. Each refers to times when people feel deeply connected with others. Love is the most powerful but least specific of these terms. Others are attached, bonded, intimate, communion, and even the word "belonging" itself. All these terms imply a celebration of "us." The thought is, "We belong together and that is wonderful." The feeling is a joyous bonding of souls. Such joinings generate loyalty because those who are joyfully bonded naturally care about each other. Although all relationships take effort to maintain and improve, the energy that goes into these unions doesn't feel like work. These relationships invigorate the participants, helping them feel more alive and vital. A joyful "us" supports a joyful "I."

The word "engrossed" best describes joyful Doing. People become engrossed with satisfying activities that demand their total attention. The activities may be called work (a particularly challenging plastic mold to design) or play (just one more level closer to expert status on the computer game). In either case, others might have to shout a few times to get the attention of someone who has become totally involved.

Activities that produce a sense of joy are always ends in themselves, not simply means to another end. Thus, the successful artist is grateful to sell their paintings not to get rich but so they can keep doing what they love. They happily spend hours and days following their path, fully realizing they are passing up opportunities to do other things.

There is a distinct but subtle difference between these joyful Doing experiences and damaging obsessions, compulsions, and addictions. The main departure is in an internal sense of ownership. People with obsessions, compulsions, and addictions feel owned by them. They are driven by these forces toward self-destructive actions that they often try to fight. They are prisoners, unable to escape their fate. In contrast, joyful engrossment doesn't feel forced. The participant is still in charge, still steering the boat. They really could stop without suffering from mental or physical withdrawal. In other words, joyful Doing occurs by invitation, while obsessions, compulsions, and addictions occur by demand.

All three joyful states bring with them a special feeling of being fully alive and completely responsive both to one's inner and outer worlds. Joy, like all emotions, is a temporary state. The goal is not to stay joyful forever. Rather, the point is that full attention to your Being, Belonging, and Doing experiences helps promote rich and satisfying periods of joy.

Shame: Defective, Rejected, Inadequate

Shame is a person's negative self-judgment. But it is also a feeling, sometimes a total body experience, that includes flushed face, weakness, nausea, and an almost unbearable need to run and hide. In my book *Letting Go of Shame*, I defined shame as, "a painful belief in one's defectiveness as a human being." This is a Being definition of shame and since then I've come to realize that there are also many Belonging and Doing aspects. Shame occurs when people sense they are failures in any of the three areas. We can be shamed about our Being (existence shame), about our inability to belong (social shame), and about our imperfect actions (competence shame).

People with Being shame feel basically defective. If you were inside the mind of a person with Being shame, here is what you'd hear: "I'm a terrible person. I'm worthless. And I'll never get better because what's wrong with me can't be fixed." Those with Being shame think they possess permanent, fatal, and irredeemable flaws. These faults may be physical (a square face, a paralyzed hand), mental (not being smart or creative enough) or emotional (depression, excessive anxiety). They may be hidden but they cannot be removed.

Friends, lovers, family, and professional counselors may tell someone with Being shame that they are just as good as anyone else. Unfortunately, these heartfelt words are usually about as effective as the Big Bad Wolf's attempts to blow down the third Little Piggie's house. The person's internal sense of despair is just too strong. "I hear what you are saying. I just don't believe it. You tell me I'm good. I agree with you intellectually. But I don't feel it. Inside I feel like rotting garbage. I stink so bad I can't stand to be around myself."

It is bad enough to feel this sense of shame at the level of Being. But shame can also occur in the area of Belonging. Then people feel exposed and rejected. It's as if everybody else can see deep inside them and hate what they see. People with Belonging shame believe that others are thinking, "Ugh . . . yuck . . . go away!" about them. They expect to be rejected by others, to be banished from the inner circle.

People with Belonging shame may go to great lengths to hide their real selves from view. Some become social chameleons, altering their appearance to please whomever they are with at the moment. Others develop false selves. They do so by rejecting completely those parts of themselves that others find unacceptable. If a parent can't tolerate aggression then a child may become passive and believe they have no anger or aggression inside them. If a parent despises generosity then that child may abandon their natural tendency to share with others. They feel the need to suppress those parts of themselves that might get them rejected from their families. Ironically, they believe they can only belong to the human race by eliminating some of their humanness.

"I'm a loser. I fail at everything I do, so why even bother trying?" Shame also has a Doing component. Deeply shamed people feel weak and inadequate. They feel ineffective, unable to do things well. This shame may affect only a small area of their lives, or it may hinder almost everything they try to do. At its worst, Doing shame may almost completely paralyze people. Overwhelmed by their sense of incompetence, they cannot even imagine starting any task.

It's hard to change your core beliefs about yourself, especially when those beliefs literally "feel" accurate. Shame is just that combination. It is a negative belief system ("I'm worthless, ugly, weak,") that produces terrible physical feelings (i.e., nausea, shaking, flushing). Shame can be alleviated, though. It takes a determined effort on the part of the shamed person who must change their internal messages. This is always a gradual process, a slow meander up the river of self-esteem, with necessary and frequent stops at such ports as First Hope and Affirmation. Sometimes the engine stops and the person floats backward for awhile, but over time people can progress far upstream. Eventually they change both their thoughts about themselves and their inner sensations. They go from feeling hopelessly bad to at least being decent human beings in their own eyes. They feel alive and well instead of sick and de-energized.

Anger: Self-Hatred, Betrayal, Frustration

✧ A fifty-year-old artist named Josefina despises herself. Full of contempt, she sneers at her pathetic attempts to be human. Asked to pretend that a doll is her, Josefina grabs it by the throat and shakes it to pieces, only wishing she could do that to herself. She says she'd kill herself in a minute if she had the guts. Josefina is consumed with self-hatred. ✧

Self-hatred is the ultimate form of Being anger. It occurs when anger at the self has become permanent and powerful. Self-haters tear themselves apart, shredding the fabric of their very Being. It's not just that they have no use for themselves. Rather, they actively want to destroy that which they consider so singularly bad.

Although you may not have experienced this depth of self-hatred, most people do experience Being anger from time to time. Perhaps you've done something "stupid" or thoughtless and you feel like kicking yourself. "I'm so dumb," you think. Right then, you have very little sympathy for yourself. You are feeling Being anger because at the time you are truly angry about who you are. But hopefully this feeling will disappear after awhile, to be replaced by your normal level of self-appreciation. Fortunately, for most people this anger is a temporary condition. It may even be useful, telling you that there is something about yourself that you need to change.

Feeling betrayed is the best word that describes Belonging anger. This feeling reflects the rage that people feel when they have been abandoned by someone they trusted. It's the adult form of protest that is first displayed by young children who sense that Mom and Dad are about to leave: "How dare you leave me! I hate you."

This type of anger only occurs between people who have depended upon each other. Lovers. Business partners. Allies. Friends. Close relatives. These are the people you expect to protect and defend you. Instead, one of them has intentionally hurt you, or at least it seems that way. You discover that a lover has been with someone else, a business partner just closed a deal with a rival, a close relative is going to testify against you in a custody fight. You feel an ancient, bestial outrage building up inside. You'd like to tear the eyes out of the skull of that person. You feel betrayed.

Jealousy is another term often associated with Belonging anger. But jealousy is really more a combination of anger and fear. The jealous person fears betrayal and so tries to guard their lover, jewels, work, etc. from the eyes and hands of perceived rivals. "Please don't leave me," frets the jealous lover. "But if you do I will be furious," adds the voice of betrayal.

Frustration is the term for Doing anger. This feeling happens because people naturally are bothered when something blocks their path. They might be upset with themselves because they're having trouble hemming a dress or tuning the car's engine. Or, like a billing clerk who cannot send out their monthly statements until the salespeople complete their reports, they might be frustrated with others. In either case, they feel like reaching out and physically removing the obstacles in their path. Sure enough, their frustration disappears when they can do that. But if they can't, their frustration may build and build until they're ready to explode.

Frustration occurs at many intensities. Annoyances are low-level frustrations. The signature of an annoyance is that it doesn't have much effect upon you even if it doesn't change. True, it's frustrating that your colleague at work whistles Dixie several times a day. But that habit has little real impact. It's only an annoyance.

The strongest form of frustration is called helpless fury or impotent rage. This feeling comes about when a person feels unable to take effective action about something exceedingly important, such as a sudden layoff notice, the discovery that their partner won't give up an affair, or endless medical bills that are driving the family into bankruptcy. The result is, "I must do something about this problem but there is nothing I can do." No wonder people experiencing helpless fury sometimes break, striking out in anger against everything and anything.

Fear: Mortal Terror, Separation Anxiety, Paralysis

✧ Denise is a forty-year-old homemaker who is scared of both life and death. Full of phobias, she fears venturing from the safety of her home. Yet she's also afraid to plunge into anything that would give substance to her life. Denise spends far too much time in her bed, numbed and frequently drugged, existing somewhere between life and death, equally terrified of both experiences. Denise cannot understand why others aren't afraid all the time like she is. ✧

Human beings have two great Being fears: the fear of death and the fear of life. Mortal terror is the literal term for our dread of death. This fear is regularly avoided by keeping busy and refusing to think about death. We also try to control the fear by going to horror movies, diminishing it through fantasy and overexposure. Still, like fog drifting in from the ocean, the fear of death gradually surrounds and engulfs us. Mortal terror cannot be escaped. It is the price we pay for awareness of our fate. The best we can do is to face our fear of death rather than avoid it.

While thoughts of death bring fear, it is equally true that we may come to fear life itself. That is when we become filled with anxiety. Life becomes scary and hard, a burden to endure rather than a joy to embrace. About all we can hope for during those times is to survive another day without anything terrible happening. Somehow we seem to have lost our courage. We have become afraid of the dynamics of life: change, growth, movement.

Being fears are thieves. They steal our ability to face both life and death.

The name for the basic Belonging fear is separation anxiety. "Please don't go. I'm afraid I'll die without you." These words might well express the feelings of a one-year-old child whose parents are trying to leave them with the babysitter. They may equally be the thoughts of an adult whose partner is leaving for the weekend or talking about ending their union.

People in relationships are tied together by many bonds, some conscious and some unconscious. It's as if a hundred ropes attach to each other. One may be called love, another neediness. The desire to take care of someone may be a third rope, a promise never to leave your partner a fourth. All of these ropes are knotted onto both parties, some more firmly than others. It is very scary to untie these knots. The fear of aloneness increases as the ropes are detached, dampening one's enthusiasm for independence. Separation anxiety strikes as each rope is unknotted, producing moments or months of panic. Unable to bear the terror, people feel desperately tempted to return to old relationships or to quickly tie the ropes to another.

A little Doing fear is certainly valuable. Such fear protects us from our own impulsivity. Maybe it's not such a great idea to climb that three-hundred-foot-high TV tower. I probably shouldn't marry that person I met last week just yet. But too much Doing fear creates paralysis, an inability to act, think, feel, and choose.

Can you remember a time when you had trouble making an important choice? Which school to attend, whom to date or marry, what job to take, where to live, whether or not to have a child, etc? Perhaps you found yourself immobilized, so afraid of making the wrong choice you couldn't act at all. You may have developed physical symptoms such as inability to sleep, shakiness, and difficulty breathing. You may have become obsessive, unable to think about anything else but unable to decide what to do. Emotionally, you probably felt trapped, smothered, desperate, and, more than anything, scared.

Physical, mental, and emotional paralysis is the ultimate product of excessive Doing fear. It is the third option when fight or flight are not possible in dangerous situations. Just stand still, like a fawn in the woods, and hope you won't be noticed. The only goal is to survive.

How do people become so afraid of Doing? One possibility is that their actions and choices may have been punished severely in the past, perhaps with physical beatings or emotional attacks. People who grow up in homes where they are not allowed to make their own choices also may, as an adult, become paralyzed with fear and doubt in the face of alternatives. There may also be problems with brain chemistry. Two psychiatric conditions that keep people from Doing freely, obsessive compulsive disorder and panic disorder, are linked to a malfunctioning brain. Fortunately, medications are now available to help people with these conditions.

Doing paralysis, however, has a more universal origin, one that applies to everybody regardless of their family or brain chemistry. The fact is that every opportunity for choice and action is a mixed blessing. Choices allow freedom. Simultaneously, though, our choices make us more responsible for our own lives. No wonder, then, that we often shy away from making choices, preferring not to disrupt the smooth flow of our lives. Instead we become avoidant, confused, and indecisive. The more we avoid, though, the less confident we feel about our ability to choose or act. The very thought of choosing becomes scary. We gradually become more and more fearful, until paralysis sets in.

Sadness: *Despairing, Sorrowful, Languishing*

Robert's marriage has been deteriorating for months now. Slowly, ever so slowly, he's become disheartened. He feels like a balloon with a slow leak in it. But what's been leaking out isn't air. It's Robert's hope that things will ever get better. Lately he's had trouble making love. It's not fun anymore, not when he and his wife argue even in bed. All in all, Robert's experiencing a slow but progressive sadness. He's just about ready to give up and get out.

Disheartened, dispirited, discouraged, dejected, despairing: all of these words describe the Being state of sadness. Each reflects a combination of mood and thought that often can be seen in sagging shoulders, drooping facial muscles, and shuffling steps. Those suffering from Being sadness must fight feelings of hopelessness and their sense that their world has fallen apart and cannot be repaired.

Emotions are usually temporary states. They tell us that something important is happening and we need to pay special attention. Thus, fear indicates the presence of imminent danger while joy indicates that something wonderful is happening right now. Sadness, too, can be short lived. Probably everybody has brief periods of sadness that quickly lift.

But sadness has another face. Of all the emotions, it most easily turns into a mood, a longer lasting feeling state. That's when being sadness turns into despair. Those in despair feel defeated by life. They become overwhelmed by their sadness. Loss of hope has permeated their Being. Despair like this initially may be associated with grieving the loss of a relationship or some other specific event. But the mood of despair lasts long after the situation has changed. It takes on a life of its own. Hopelessness leads to helplessness. People become so trapped in despair that sadness threatens to become their permanent state. Despair, a mood, can even trigger the physiological changes in body and brain that produce depression.

"Sorrow" is a term that signifies Belonging sadness. It's the sadness due to the loss of something loved. Sorrow is a form of loyalty. It reminds us of the importance of the now broken connection. It tells others that the deceased or lost individual has been deeply loved and will be remembered in heart and mind. Sorrow is also a kind of protest: "How can you leave me to face the world alone?" That's why anger may be added to sadness during grieving.

Belonging sadness is relieved through the process of grieving, although sorrow, like other forms of sadness, may turn into a long term mood that defies change. Sorrow can even become emotionally addictive, bittersweet in its validation of a broken bond. Indeed, perpetual grieving can maintain a relationship in one's mind long after the bond has been severed in the real world. The cost of endless sorrow is that one cannot develop new relationships.

Deep sadness can shut down a person to the point where even their normal actions are affected. First comes a melancholy feeling, a pensive downswing of the spirit, the kind of state in which you gaze for long hours out the window while seeing nothing at all. That's followed or accompanied by languor, a word that refers to a process of becoming weakened by sadness, a listlessness based upon loss. Together, melancholy and languor combine to inhibit action.

This Doing sadness may produce what Emma Gut calls a productive depression. These temporary and useful depressions are often mistakenly diagnosed as organic depressions. Like organic depression, productive depressions hinder people from pursuing their normal activities. But unlike organic depressions, productive depressions often lift quickly once the source of the person's anguish can be determined.

⬦ Take Ellie, for example; she has placed the desire for financial security too far ahead of her need for creativity. Hanging onto a thoroughly unsatisfying job, Ellie tries to be happy. Gradually, though, her Doing sadness takes over, making it harder and harder for her to get up in the morning to go to work. Her unconscious is giving her a strong message: "Hold on there, Ellie. You're not going anywhere until you deal with what you're missing. You're not doing what you most need to do. That's why you're unhappy." Ellie's depression will end once she gets the message and either changes jobs or finds other ways to be creative. ✧

Exercises to Help You Understand Your Emotions

Exercise—Envisioning Your Joy

- If your joy were a color, what color would it be?

- If your joy were a landscape painting, what would the scene be?

- If your joy were a season, which one would it be?

- If your joy were a song, what would be its name and lyrics?

- If your joy were a gift, what would it be? To whom would you give the gift of your joy?

Exercise—Creating the Possibility for Joy

Joy cannot be willed. You can't just make it happen. But you can increase the opportunities for bliss, intimacy, and engrossment. What can you do to make joy a greater part of your life? Make a list of at least five things to start with and try to integrate these things into your life.

Exercise—Identifying Shame Experiences

Identify one experience that left you feeling: that you could or should not be; that you could or should never belong; that you could or should not complete a job or experience. How are these experiences similar and/or different from each other? Could you use one of these experiences to understand yourself better now? How?

Exercise—Self-Hatred, Self-Forgiveness, and Self-Acceptance

Self-hatred is the ultimate form of Being anger. It occurs when you find yourself despising everything about you. You can find virtually nothing worth appreciating about yourself when you are full of self-hate.

There are two antidotes for self-hatred. The first is self-forgiveness, which entails dealing with the things you have done that make you feel guilty. Self-forgiveness involves acknowledging your faults and the things you've done to hurt others and yourself. It may mean you need to make a list of who you have harmed and make amends to them if you can. Self-forgiveness also requires that you make an honest commitment to live a better life, one in which you honor yourself and others by living up to your beliefs and values. Once you've made this commitment, you can make a conscious decision to forgive yourself so that you can go on with your life. You can forgive yourself for your transgressions and be proud of your current conduct.

Self-acceptance deals more with shame than guilt. Here you must recognize your natural limitations and weaknesses as a human being. Self-acceptance involves taking in five personal messages: I am good, I am good enough, I belong, I am loved, and I am (Potter-Efron and Potter-Efron 1989).

What do you need to do today to begin or continue the process of self-forgiving? Of self-acceptance? Take the time to write down a concrete plan that can help you renew your life.

Exercise—Small Fears

Mortal terror, separation anxiety, paralysis: these are strong terms for strong situations. But what about the small fears that percolate through your brain, the sometimes nameless anxieties that leave you shaken without reason, the habitual worries over money, image, etc. that lie in wait, the annoying timidities like fear of heights that impede your activities?

Make a list of these small Being, Belonging, and Doing fears on one side of a piece of paper. On the other side note how they affect you and limit your life. Now pick one or two to challenge. Decide exactly what you need to do to reduce that fear.

Then do whatever you most need to do so that your life will be less constricted by your small fears.

Exercise—The Sounds of Sadness

Chanting or wailing seems to be a nearly universal way to deal with sadness. Somehow the melodic repetition of musical or verbal phrases provides a measure of comfort and security.

What sounds, words, phrases, or tones constitute your sadness chant? Try singing aloud your sadness, alone or with others.

Exercise—Hearing the Message in Your Sadness

Your sadness may have one or more important messages for you, especially if you have felt so overwhelmed with sadness that it's hard for you to function. Imagine your sadness as a friend sitting beside you, perhaps the two of you embracing and comforting each other. "Please listen to me," says your friend. "I've been trying so hard to tell you something important and all you've done is to try to ignore me." This time agree to really listen to your sadness. Take some time to listen quietly for the message. What does it tell you?

Joy, sadness, anger, and all of our other emotions are clearly connected with the concepts of Being, Belonging, and Doing. The more awareness we have of them, the better we can identify and name our feelings. To know, for instance, that you are not just experiencing sadness but that the sadness is about Belonging and is called sorrow may help you complete a necessary grieving process.

We have now discussed in detail the general nature of the Being, Belonging, and Doing experiences. In the next and concluding chapter, you will have an opportunity to look deeply into your own Being, Belonging, and Doing needs and to make plans for the future that will help you in all three areas.

Chapter Eight

Weaving Your Personal Tapestry: Your Personal Relationship with Being, Belonging, and Doing

You are the Weaver

Return to the image of Being, Belonging, and Doing as three differently colored and textured fabrics. Purple, yellow, red. Smooth, bumpy, soft. Imagine these fabrics just laying on the floor, waiting. They're waiting for you to notice them, for you to pick them up and play with them. They're ready for you to weave them into a rich, beautiful, unique tapestry.

You are the weaver. Certainly, though, you will need time and patience to plan your design. Also, you'll probably want to study the fabrics for awhile before you start. That's what the rest of this chapter is for. In it there are three extensive exercises that can help you understand your past, present, and future relationships with Being, Belonging, and Doing.

First, the Being, Belonging, and Doing Self-Discovery Quiz will help you discover your current relationship with these three life needs. Then, the Being, Belonging, and Doing Personal History Time Lines will help you find how the themes of Being, Belonging, and Doing have been running through the whole history of your life. Finally, the Being, Belonging, and Doing Goals List will help you decide what goals to set in the near future.

These three exercises are tools that will help you better craft your tapestry. But you are completely in charge. Use them if they're helpful. Put them aside if they're not.

Exercise—Being, Belonging, and Doing Self-Discovery Quiz

Score each of the following items from 0–10 points.

0 = This item is completely untrue for me.

10 = This item is completely true for me.

Example: A score of "7" on "My life has meaning and purpose" would mean that this statement is mostly but not completely true for you.

	A	B	C
1. My life has meaning and purpose.	——		
2. I greatly enjoy the times I share with others.		——	
3. All in all, I feel quite capable and competent.			——
4. I feel prepared and unafraid about my death.	——		
5. I trust that people who leave me for awhile will want to return.		——	
6. I move towards the problems I face in life instead of avoiding them.			——
7. I make difficult choices, even those that greatly affect my life.	——		
8. The people in my life help me feel complete and whole.		——	
9. My goal is to be "good enough" rather than perfect.			——
10. I fully accept myself as a human being.	——		

	A	B	C
11. I regularly share my thoughts and feelings with others.		___	
12. I am good at what really matters to me.			___
13. I feel full of life, energy, and vigor.	___		
14. I feel comfortable saying the words, "I belong."		___	
15. I accept praise comfortably when it is offered.			___
16. The life I lead reflects my real wants and needs.	___		
17. I seldom feel overwhelmed or swallowed up by others.		___	
18. I recognize, but don't exaggerate, my weaknesses and limitations.			___
19. I regularly seek privacy to think about what is important in my life.	___		
20. I feel loved and lovable.		___	
21. I never engage in "self-sabotage" behaviors that keep me from succeeding.			___
22. "I am" is good enough for me—I don't have to justify my existence.	___		
23. I belong to groups and organizations outside my immediate family.		___	
24. I am good both at starting and finishing tasks.			___
25. I accept the unique aspects of myself that make me different than others.	___		
26. I feel connected spiritually with something greater than myself.		___	
27. I keep going when I decide to do something, even if I do poorly at first.			___

	A	**B**	**C**

28. I am curious and interested in myself—who I am and who I am becoming.   _____

29. I truly believe I have a place in this world.   _____

30. I know when enough is enough—when to stop working or Doing.   _____

Column A is your Being score. Add all of the items in column A (the first question in each set of three: items 1, 4, 7, etc.). Your Being score = _____

Column B is your Belonging score. Add all of the items in column B (the second question in each set of three: items 2, 5, 8, etc.). Your Belonging score = _____

Column C is your Doing score. Add all of the items in column C (the third question in each set of three: items 3, 6, 9, etc.). Your Doing score = _____

The total of all three is your BBD (Being, Belonging, and Doing) score. Your BBD score = _____

Interpreting Your Scores

Your Scores for Individual Items

Low scores on any single item (5 points or less) tell you where you have the greatest immediate potential for change. For example, if you scored low on item 19 ("I regularly seek privacy to think about what is important in my life"), then perhaps you'll want to start carving out some alone time right away.

Your Scores for Each Column

The maximum score for each column is 100 points. You are doing pretty well in each area if your score is 75 or higher. A score below 50 is an invitation for you to pay more attention to that part of your life. Even high scores, however, don't mean you should ignore that area. There's always work to be done. And don't feel hopeless or ashamed if your scores are low. That's just an invitation for you to think seriously about how you can improve your life in these spheres.

The lowest score of your three columns (A = Being, B = Belonging, C = Doing) tells you which major need has been most neglected. Your life will be more complete when you take some time to explore that area.

The difference between columns is also important. A very high score in one area accompanied by lower scores in the others may mean that your life is out of balance. You may be an "overdoer," for example, if you score 92 points on Doing but only 60 or 70 on Being and Belonging. One goal is to achieve balance in the orchestra of your life, so that all the instruments are well-tuned and well-played.

Your Total Score

There is a possible score of 300 points if you add together all three columns. All in all a score of 225 is very positive, indicating that you are probably doing well with your whole life. A score below 150 may be cause for concern.

Look closely at the Being column. Is your score as high as you'd like? Are there particular questions that point to areas you could explore? What would your score have been last year? Ten years ago? What about Being, *your* Being, most fascinates you? Who are you? Who are you becoming?

Scan the questions in the Belonging column. Are you satisfied with your answers? How important is Belonging in your life? Think of the times you've most felt you belonged and the times you've felt most isolated and apart. How have these times affected you? If you have difficulty with Belonging, are there any questions that can help you see what to work on?

Look over the Doing column. Do you see any patterns in your answers that you need to attend to? Are there certain questions that stand out and give you immediate direction? All in all, how are you Doing?

This quiz is meant as a guide, not a criticism. It's important that you use it to notice your opportunities for growth rather than to beat yourself up for not being perfect on all three scales. The most important question you can ask yourself here is this: "What new directions can my life take that could help me feel better connected with my Being, Belonging, and Doing needs?"

Exercise—Being, Belonging, and Doing
Personal History Time Lines

The goal of this exercise is to help you clarify your sense of how you have experienced Being, Belonging, and Doing during your lifetime by creating three separate time lines, one each for Being, Belonging, and Doing.

First, you will need to gather some blank paper for this exercise. Turn each page sideways and mark in several consecutive years, starting at the first year of the time period you're looking for (e.g., 20 ——— 21 ——— 22 ——— 23 ——— 24 . . .). You will need three sets of this time line, one each for Being, Belonging, and Doing.

The idea is to fill in specific events or circumstances that illuminate your relationship to Being, Belonging, or Doing over the years. You may want to do this by thinking about a particular period in your life, say your twenties, and then filling in all you remember about the three areas during that time. You may want to start by thinking about one of the three areas throughout your life, perhaps beginning with the one area you feel most clear about. Or you may just want to let your memories guide you randomly through all three areas at once.

Here is a sample time line fragment from a fifty-year-old man:

Being: age ——— 21 ——— 22 ——— 23 ——— 24 ——— 25 ——— 26 ——— 27 ———
    my "wounded   friend died: used LSD as a
    soul" era: first real   spiritual quest
    mostly a game   awareness of
                   mortality

Belonging: age ——— 21 ——— 22 ——— 23 ——— 24 ——— 25 ——— 26 ——— 27 ———
                 first love: felt very
                 confusion and   lonely and
                 merger   unwanted

Doing: age ——— 21 ——— 22 ——— 23 ——— 24 ——— 25 ——— 26 ——— 27 ———
    graduated from   fired from   my "incompetent"
    college   first job   period: couldn't
                 for being   do anything right
                 lazy—shocked

Being issues are often about: life and death; major decisions; becoming aware of your most important wants and needs; trying on particular identities; the quest for authenticity (personal honesty with oneself); periods of solitude; the search for meaning in life; and deeply personal spiritual times.

Belonging issues are frequently about: periods of connection with others; losses, abandonments, betrayals; periods of spiritual communion; memberships in groups and organizations; important times with family; friendship; periods of loneliness; grieving; and bonding.

Doing concerns are often about: tasks completed and not completed; seeking a spiritually meaningful "calling"; career choices; feeling and behaving in competent or incompetent ways; successes and failures; working and overworking; hobbies and recreational pursuits; and moving towards or away from opportunity.

Take your time with this history. In fact, you may want to keep these charts around for awhile, adding to them as you remember more.

Look for patterns as you work on your personal history. Are there periods, for instance, mostly filled with Being issues? With Belonging? With Doing? Are there times when all three are nicely connected? Are there blank spots on your time lines when nothing much seemed to have happened in any area? If you were to divide your life by decades (or five-year blocks if you're younger) what would you notice? Most importantly, is there evidence that you have neglected one or more areas over the length of your lifetime? If so, it's not too late to begin attending more consciously to that area.

Exercise—Setting Being, Belonging, and Doing Goals

It is both possible and desirable to set conscious goals in the areas of Being, Belonging, and Doing. In this section, there is a list of possible problems and goals in each area. The list, though, is far from complete. You may think of many other goals not listed.

Look over the list. Choose one or two goals for each area, from either the list or your own ideas, so that you end up with a total of three to six goals. These are the areas you are choosing to focus upon in the immediate future, say the next three months.

Once you have chosen the goals, take some time to operationalize them. In other words, ask yourself exactly what you need to do to reach each goal or at least to move in that direction. What will you be doing, thinking, or feeling differently three months from now as a result of working towards these goals? What must you do immediately to get started? Make sure you're setting reasonable and doable goals.

Keep your goal sheet with or near you. Consult it regularly. Are you reaching your goals? If not, what might you do differently? If so, what have you been doing that you want to continue? Review the entire list after three months. You may want to stay focused on these goals a while longer. Or perhaps it may be time to select some new ones.

Being Problems and Goals

- Problem: Uncertainty about your identity.
  Goal: To gain a greater awareness of who you are: your interests, values, etc.

- Problem: Feeling phony, false, or fraudulent.
  Goal: Discover your real self—the person you are when you're not playing roles or pleasing others.

- Problem: Fear of or avoidance of the topic of death.
  Goal: Address both the fear issue and mortality itself.

- Problem: Life feels meaningless, without direction or purpose.
  Goal: Seek out your deeper goals and act to live by them.

- Problem: Avoidance of alone time (loneliness anxiety).
  Goal: Become comfortable with yourself.

- Problem: Feeling depleted and de-energized, having a loss of vigor.
  Goal: Discover physical or emotional sources of energy loss and correct.

- Problem: Need to "earn" the right to exist (by taking care of others, accomplishing, etc.).
  Goal: Self-acceptance (Being is enough).

- Problem: Going through life on "automatic pilot," not noticing your real choices.
  Goal: Increased awareness of the choices you have in your life.

- Problem: Lack of curiosity or wonder about yourself.
  Goal: Increased awareness and interest in yourself.

- Problem: Excessive need for affirmation or attention.
  Goal: Learn sources of need, learn to soothe and comfort yourself.

- Problem: Inability to accept others' interest, attention, or appreciation.
  Goal: Learn to accept attention without excessive discomfort.

- Problem: Self-neglect (poor nutrition, lack of sleep, failure to get needed attention, etc.).
  Goal: Improved self-worth to the point of regularly taking care of your own needs.

- Problem: Self-destructiveness (mutilation, addiction, suicidality, etc.).
  Goal: Increased desire to exist, acceptance of your Being.

- Problem: Cannot sense your inner spirituality.
  Goal: Find a spiritual connection with something greater than yourself.

Belonging Problems and Goals

- Problem: Fear of abandonment.
  Goal: Deal with history of abandonment, change self-talk that predicts abandonment.

- Problem: Sense of never really Belonging.
  Goal: Develop a true sense of Belonging, accept the opportunities to belong that already exist or come your way.

- Problem: Excessive independence (refusal to need others).
  Goal: Movement toward interdependence (mutual vulnerability and cooperation).

- Problem: Feeling unloved or unwanted.
  Goal: Assess reality of situation. If unrealistic, challenge irrational belief system.

- Problem: Excessive compliance (constantly doing what others want in order to be accepted, even if you want to do otherwise).
  Goal: Deal with fears of unacceptability to become more assertive.

- Problem: Rapid, unselective bonding that produces poor relationships.
  Goal: Slow down the bonding process, become more selective.

- Problem: Relationship avoidance (too slow, overly selective bonding).
  Goal: Improved bonding process, become less critical.

- Problem: Excessive loyalty even when the loyalty is not deserved or has been misused.
  Goal: Practice the art of "letting go" emotionally and physically.

- Problem: Spiritual isolation.
  Goal: Find groups or organizations in which you can experience a feeling of communion. Address your need for personal connection with a force greater than yourself.

- Problem: Inability to share thoughts and feelings with others.
  Goal: Practice more self-disclosure.

- Problem: Isolation from family, community, etc.
  Goal: More active involvement in these areas.

- Problem: Clinging dependency (inability to let others go).
  Goal: Learn to tolerate and accept both temporary and permanent losses.

Doing Problems and Goals

- Problem: Feeling generally incapable and incompetent.
  Goal: Increased general sense of competence.

- Problem: Feeling unjustifiably limited or incompetent in a specific area.
  Goal: Gain a more realistic appreciation of your skills in that area.

- Problem: Grandiosity (feeling more competent than you really are, in a particular area or in general).
  Goal: Challenge grandiosity as a defense against inner feelings of inadequacy by dealing with those feelings.

- Problem: Avoidance of psychologically threatening tasks, challenges, and opportunities.
  Goal: Learn coping response patterns (moving towards challenges instead of away from them).

- Problem: Giving up too quickly in the face of failure or frustration.
  Goal: Redefine failure as a necessary step towards success, gain ability to tolerate and learn from failure.

- Problem: Lack of initiative (inability to start activities).
  Goal: Increased ability to initiate activities.

- Problem: Inability to complete activities.
  Goal: Improved follow-through as measured by number of completed tasks.

- Problem: Self-sabotage.
  Goal: Discover and challenge sources of self-sabotage, break self-sabotaging routines.

- Problem: Impostor syndrome (feel like a fake in major roles, even though you are actually competent and qualified).
  Goal: Accept self as competent in those roles.

- Problem: Inability to accept praise or appreciation for task performance.
  Goal: Learn to accept and take in praise.

- Problem: Compulsive overdoing (inability to stop).
  Goal: Discover reasons for overdoing, practice appropriate self-care.

- Problem: Personal sense of identity is overly dependent upon work and activity ("I am = "What I do").
  Goal: To balance Doing with Being and Belonging.

- Problem: Perfectionism.
  Goal: Accept the principle of being "good enough."

- Problem: Meaningless task performance (your Doing seems meaningless, pointless, irrelevant, or useless).
  Goal: Seek activities that are meaningful—possible callings.

What to Do with Your Goals

Selecting goals to help you get better in touch with your Being, Belonging, and Doing needs is a good first step. But remember that it takes five steps to turn wishes into wants and dreams into reality. Those five steps are choosing, planning, starting, following

Being, Belonging, Doing

through, and finishing. Choosing is what you've just completed. To complete the process, you need to go through the next four steps. Refer back to chapter 4 for a review of these steps; they can help you turn your choices into a concrete, doable plan.

Achieving Balance

A teeter-totter would be just a long plank without its fulcrum, its balance point. So too are the concepts of Being, Belonging, and Doing diminished when they are out of balance. Seeking balance is a way to achieve harmony among these three powerful forces. However, the balance needed here cannot be a static single point, such as a fulcrum. People are much more complex, with more than two sides to balance. Since we are constantly changing, our balance points must change with us.

Balance never just happens. It is a conscious process. You must deliberately seek to integrate your Being, Belonging, and Doing needs, resisting the tendencies to ignore or overdevelop any one of them. And, no matter how successful you've been, periodically you have to review and rebalance the system, just as even the best cars need occasional tune-ups and repairs.

The reward for this periodic maintenance is well worth the effort. An integrated life simply feels better than one out of balance. A day that includes taking time for yourself, connecting with others, and participating in meaningful activities is intrinsically satisfying. Contrast that with a day spent entirely alone, or one totally relationship centered, or one spent in compulsive overactivity. True, some of these days may be necessary. Some may be sought, usually because an area has been neglected so long that it demands undivided attention. In the long run, though, those days spent honoring all three forces will simply feel best.

Vision

People move most confidently when they have a clear vision of their desired future. The person who sees a clear path ahead walks purposefully forward, while others take small, tentative steps through the fog that surrounds them.

That's why it's important that you take the time to visualize your Being, Belonging, and Doing future. Let that fog of doubt and indecision disperse, if only for a few minutes. Blow it out of your mind by focussing upon what you most want in life.

When you can see ahead, think about these questions:

- Who am I becoming?

- With whom do I most want to share my life?

- What can I do that will most fill me with joy?

- What will my life be like a year from now if I keep going just the way I am? How will it look and feel a year from now if I add more Being, Belonging, or Doing? If I take away some Being, Belonging, or Doing?

- If I really honor all three forces, how will my life change in the next year?

Some Final Words

I have tried to present in this book a simple and straightforward model of three basic human needs. My hope is that reading this book and applying the concepts to your life will help you say three things to yourself:

I am. I exist. I celebrate my Being.

I belong. I have a place in this world.

I can do things well. I am competent.

Being, Belonging, and Doing are paths without end. They last a lifetime, always changing, never completely predictable. It's all too easy to lose the trail, though, and that is when our lives become frustrating and seem meaningless. Fortunately, it's always possible to pick up these trails. They are so deeply part of human nature that they cannot be misplaced forever.

The three paths of Being, Belonging, and Doing constantly cross and weave around each other. Sometimes they run side by side, sometimes they appear to go off in very different directions. Ultimately, they all lead towards a place of safety, peace, contentment, and serenity.

Walking the paths of Being, Belonging, and Doing is a life-long challenge. Hopefully, reading this book has helped you see these trails more clearly, helped you cut through some of the brush, perhaps even assisted you in finding a clearing where all the paths have joined for awhile. May your life be full of rich and interesting trails, and may you have the courage to follow them to their ends.

References

Ainsworth, M. 1982. "Attachment: Retrospect and Prospect." In *The Place of Attachment in Human Behavior*, edited by C. M. Parkes and J. Sterenson-Parkes. New York: Basic Books.

Bowlby, J. 1982. "Attachment and Loss: Retrospect and Prospect." *American Journal of Orthopsychiatry*. 52: 664–678.

Davis, M., E. Robbins Eshelman, and M. McKay. 1995. *The Relaxation and Stress Reduction Workbook*. 4th ed. Oakland, Calif.: New Harbinger Publications.

Gibran, K. 1973. *The Prophet*. New York: Knopf.

Gut, E. 1989. *Productive and Unproductive Depression*. New York: Basic Books.

Johnson, S. M. 1994. *Character Styles*. New York: W. W. Norton.

Kaufman, G. 1989. *The Psychology of Shame*. New York: Springer.

Korb, M., J. Gorell, and V. Vanderect. 1989. *Gestalt Therapy: Practice and Theory*. 2d ed. New York: Pergamon Press.

Lankton, S. 1989. *Tales of Enchantment: Goal-Oriented Metaphors for Adults in Therapy*. New York: Brunner/Mazel.

Masters, J. 1985. *The Real Self: A Developmental, Self, and Object Relations Approach*. New York: Brunner/Mazel.

Moore, T. 1992. *Care of the Soul.* New York: Harper Collins.

Potter-Efron, P., and R. Potter-Efron. 1989. *Letting Go of Shame.* Center City, Minn.: Hazelden Publications.

Potter-Efron, P., and R. Potter-Efron. 1995. *Letting Go of Anger: The Ten Most Common Anger Styles and What to Do About Them.* Oakland, Calif.: New Harbinger Publications.

Progoff, Ira. 1992. *At a Journal Workshop.* Revised ed. New York: Putnam.

Smedes, Lewis. 1993. *Shame and Grace: Healing the Shame We Don't Deserve.* San Francisco: Harper Collins.

Weber, Max. 1958. *The Protestant Ethic and the Spirit of Capitalism.* New York: Charles Scribner's Sons.

Whitfield, C. 1984. "Stress Management and Spirituality During Recovery: A Transpersonal Approach. Part II: Being." *Alcoholism Treatment Quarterly.* Vol. 1. 2: 1–50.

Winnicott, D. W. 1958. *Collected Papers.* London: Tavistock.

Yalom, I. 1980. *Existential Psychotherapy.* New York: Basic Books.

Yalom, I. 1989. *Love's Executioner and Other Tales of Psychotherapy.* New York: Basic Books.

More New Harbinger Titles

ANGRY ALL THE TIME
An Emergency Guide to Anger Control

Ron Potter-Efron's emergency guide to changing anger-provoking thoughts, dealing with old resentments, asking for what you want without anger, and staying calm one day at a time.
Item ALL Paperback, $12.95

LETTING GO OF ANGER

Ron helps you recognize the ten destructive ways that people deal with anger and identify which anger styles may be undermining your personal and work relationships.
Item LET Paperback, $13.95

ILLUMINATING THE HEART
Steps Toward a More Spiritual Marriage

Outlines steps that couples can take to examine fundamental beliefs, search for shared meaning and purpose, and reconnect to each other, their families, and the wider community.
Item LUM Paperback, $13.95

THE DAILY RELAXER

Distills the best of the best to bring together the most effective and popular techniques for learning how to relax.
Item DALY Paperback, $12.95

DON'T TAKE IT PERSONALLY
The Art of Dealing with Rejection

Reveals the power of negative childhood messages and shows how to depersonalize responses, establish boundaries, and develop a new sense of self-acceptance and self-confidence.
Item DOTA Paperback, $12.95

Call **toll-free 1-800-748-6273** to order. Have your Visa or Mastercard number ready. Or send a check for the titles you want to New Harbinger Publications, 5674 Shattuck Avenue, Oakland, CA 94609. Include $3.80 for the first book and 75¢ for each additional book to cover shipping and handling. (California residents please include appropriate sales tax.) Allow four to six weeks for delivery.

Prices subject to change without notice.

Some Other New Harbinger Self-Help Titles

The Headache & Neck Pain Workbook, $14.95
Perimenopause, $13.95
The Self-Forgiveness Handbook, $12.95
A Woman's Guide to Overcoming Sexual Fear and Pain, $14.95
Mind Over Malignancy, $12.95
Scarred Soul, $13.95
The Angry Heart, $13.95
Don't Take It Personally, $12.95
Becoming a Wise Parent For Your Grown Child, $12.95
Clear Your Past, Change Your Future, $12.95
Preparing for Surgery, $17.95
Coming Out Everyday, $13.95
Ten Things Every Parent Needs to Know, $12.95
The Power of Two, $12.95
It's Not OK Anymore, $13.95
The Daily Relaxer, $12.95
The Body Image Workbook, $17.95
Living with ADD, $17.95
Taking the Anxiety Out of Taking Tests, $12.95
The Taking Charge of Menopause Workbook, $17.95
Living with Angina, $12.95
PMS: Women Tell Women How to Control Premenstrual Syndrome, $13.95
Five Weeks to Healing Stress: The Wellness Option, $17.95
Choosing to Live: How to Defeat Suicide Through Cognitive Therapy, $12.95
Why Children Misbehave and What to Do About It, $14.95
Illuminating the Heart, $13.95
When Anger Hurts Your Kids, $12.95
The Addiction Workbook, $17.95
The Chronic Pain Control Workbook, Second Edition, $17.95
Fibromyalgia & Chronic Myofascial Pain Syndrome, $19.95
Flying Without Fear, $12.95
Kid Cooperation: How to Stop Yelling, Nagging & Pleading and Get Kids to Cooperate, $12.95
Conquering Carpal Tunnel Syndrome and Other Repetitive Strain Injuries, $17.95
The Tao of Conversation, $12.95
An End to Panic: Breakthrough Techniques for Overcoming Panic Disorder, $17.95
Living Without Procrastination: How to Stop Postponing Your Life, $12.95
Letting Go of Anger: The 10 Most Common Anger Styles and What to Do About Them, $12.95
Messages: The Communication Skills Workbook, Second Edition, $13.95
The Anxiety & Phobia Workbook, Second Edition, $17.95
The Relaxation & Stress Reduction Workbook, Fourth Edition, $17.95
Living Without Depression & Manic Depression: A Workbook for Maintaining Mood Stability, $17.95
Visualization for Change, Second Edition, $13.95
Postpartum Survival Guide, $13.95
Angry All the Time: An Emergency Guide to Anger Control, $12.95
Couple Skills: Making Your Relationship Work, $13.95
Self-Esteem, Second Edition, $13.95
I Can't Get Over It, A Handbook for Trauma Survivors, Second Edition, $15.95
Dying of Embarrassment: Help for Social Anxiety and Social Phobia, $12.95
The Depression Workbook: Living With Depression and Manic Depression, $17.95
Men & Grief: A Guide for Men Surviving the Death of a Loved One, $13.95
When Once Is Not Enough: Help for Obsessive Compulsives, $13.95
The Three Minute Meditator, Third Edition, $12.95
Beyond Grief: A Guide for Recovering from the Death of a Loved One, $13.95
Hypnosis for Change: A Manual of Proven Techniques, Third Edition, $13.95
When Anger Hurts, $13.95

Call **toll free, 1-800-748-6273,** to order. Have your Visa or Mastercard number ready. Or send a check for the titles you want to New Harbinger Publications, Inc., 5674 Shattuck Ave., Oakland, CA 94609. Include $3.80 for the first book and 75¢ for each additional book, to cover shipping and handling. (California residents please include appropriate sales tax.) Allow four to six weeks for delivery.

Prices subject to change without notice.